The Dreyfus Affair

The Dreyfus Affair

LESLIE DERFLER

Greenwood Guides to Historic Events, 1500–1900
Linda S. Frey and Marsha L. Frey, Series Editors

GREENWOOD PRESS
Westport, Connecticut • London

Library of Congress Cataloging-in-Publication Data

Derfler, Leslie.
  The Dreyfus affair / Leslie Derfler.
     p. cm.—(Greenwood guides to historic events, 1500–1900, ISSN 1538–442X)
  Includes bibliographical references and index.
  ISBN 0–313–31791–7 (alk. paper)
    1. Dreyfus, Alfred, 1859–1935. 2. France—Politics and government—1870–1940.
  I. Title. II. Series.
DC354.D38 2002
944.081′2′092—dc21   2001038365

British Library Cataloguing in Publication Data is available.

Library of Congress Catalog Card Number: 2001038365
ISBN: 0–313–31791–7
ISSN: 1538–442X

First published in 2002

Greenwood Press, 88 Post Road West, Westport, CT 06881
An imprint of Greenwood Publishing Group, Inc.
www.greenwood.com

Printed in the United States of America

The paper used in this book complies with the
Permanent Paper Standard issued by the National
Information Standards Organization (Z39.48–1984).

10 9 8 7 6 5 4 3 2 1

Copyright Acknowledgments

The author and publisher gratefully acknowledge permission for use of the following
material:

Extracts from Jean-Denis Bredin, *The Affair: The Case of Alfred Dreyfus* (New York:
George Braziller, 1986). Used by permission of George Braziller Publishers.

Extracts from Arthur Hertzberg, *The Zionist Idea* (New York: Doubleday, 1959).
Copyright © 1959 by Arthur Hertzberg. Used by permission of Doubleday, a division
of Random House, Inc.

CONTENTS

   Photo essay follows page 63.

SERIES FOREWORD

American statesman Adlai Stevenson stated that "We can chart our future clearly and wisely only when we know the path which has led to the present." This series, Greenwood Guides to Historic Events, 1500–1900, is designed to illuminate that path by focusing on events from 1500 to 1900 that have shaped the world. The years 1500 to 1900 include what historians call the Early Modern Period (1500 to 1789, the onset of the French Revolution) and part of the modern period (1789 to 1900).

In 1500, an acceleration of key trends marked the beginnings of an interdependent world and the posing of seminal questions that changed the nature and terms of intellectual debate. The series closes with 1900, the inauguration of the twentieth century. This period witnessed profound economic, social, political, cultural, religious, and military changes. An industrial and technological revolution transformed the modes of production, marked the transition from a rural to an urban economy, and ultimately raised the standard of living. Social classes and distinctions shifted. The emergence of the territorial and later the national state altered man's relations with and view of political authority. The shattering of the religious unity of the Roman Catholic world in Europe marked the rise of a new pluralism. Military revolutions changed the nature of warfare. The books in this series emphasize the complexity and diversity of the human tapestry and include political, economic, social, intellectual, military, and cultural topics. Some of the authors focus on events in U.S. history such as the Salem Witchcraft Trials, the American Revolution, the abolitionist movement, and the Civil War. Others analyze European topics, such as the Reformation and Counter Reformation and the French Revolution. Still others bridge cultures and continents by examining the voyages of discovery, the Atlantic slave trade, and the Age of Imperialism. Some focus on intellectual questions that have shaped the modern world, such as Darwin's *Origin of Species*, or on turning points such as the Age of Romanticism. Others examine defining economic, religious, or legal events or issues such as the building of the railroads, the Second Great Awakening, and abolitionism. Heroes (e.g., Lewis and Clark), scientists (e.g., Darwin), military leaders (e.g., Napoleon), poets (e.g., Bryron), stride across its pages. Many of these events were seminal in that they marked profound changes or turning points. The scientific revolution, for example, changed the way individuals viewed themselves and their world.

The authors, acknowledged experts in their fields, synthesize key events, set developments within the larger historical context and, most important, present a well-balanced, well-written account that integrates the most recent scholarship in the field.

The topics were chosen by an advisory board composed of historians, high school history teachers, and school librarians to support the curriculum and meet student research needs. The volumes are designed to serve as resources for student research and to provide clearly written interpretations of topics central to the secondary school and lower-level undergraduate history curriculum. Each author outlines a basic chronology to guide the reader through often confusing events and a historical overview to set those events within a narrative framework. Three to five topical chapters underscore critical aspects of the event. In the final chapter the author examines the impact and consequences of the event. Biographical sketches furnish background on the lives and contributions of the players who strut across this stage. Ten to fifteen primary documents ranging from letters to diary entries, song lyrics, proclamations, and posters, cast light on the event, provide material for student essays, and stimulate a critical engagement with the sources. Introductions identify the authors of the documents and the main issues. In some cases a glossary of selected terms is provided as a guide to the reader. Each work contains an annotated bibliography of recommended books, articles, CD-ROMs, Internet sites, videos, and films that set the materials within the historical debate.

These works will lead to a more sophisticated understanding of the events and debates that have shaped the modern world and will stimulate a more active engagement with the issues that still affect us. It has been a particularly enriching experience to work closely with such dedicated professionals. We have come to know and value even more highly the authors in this series and our editors at Greenwood, particularly Barbara Rader and Kevin Ohe. In many cases they have become more than colleagues, they have become friends. To them and to future historians we dedicate this series.

Linda S. Frey
University of Montana

Marsha L. Frey
Kansas State University

PREFACE

The Dreyfus Affair, which took place at the end of the nineteenth and the beginning of the twentieth centuries, was technically and legally the trial, conviction, and deportation of a French army officer on the charge of selling military secrets to the German government; the subsequent reopening of the case, with his retrial, reconviction, and immediate pardon; and later, still another reopening and review with the complete vindication of the accused. All this took twelve years.

The Affair, however, can be considered in a number of ways. The long and difficult struggle of the early Dreyfusards (those who supported Dreyfus) to expose the officer they believed to be the real culprit makes the most thrilling and fantastic of detective stories. The division across existing alignments of almost all France into two hostile camps—those who demanded revision of the case and those determined to prevent it, those who attached supreme value to justice for the individual and those who would subordinate him to the best interests of the state—provides perhaps the perfect, and certainly the clearest, case history of the moral crisis undergone by a nation. We have, furthermore, a now-classic illustration of the battle for supremacy waged within a republic between its civil and military powers, as well as the plainest presentation of the arguments used by both sides. And from an intellectual and literary point of view, the Affair served as the experience of an entire generation.

The anti-Semitism that persuaded the military of the culpability of a Jewish officer when an act of treason was discovered, influenced two guilty verdicts by courts-martial, and accounted for mob action, the birth of anti-Jewish para-military organizations, and attempted coups, portended the totalitarianism struggling to be born and contributed to the creation of a Zionist (Jewish nationalist) solution. Finally and very important, it must be taken as a decisive episode in the political history of modern France.

The conflict that lay at the heart of the Affair—that between the demands of national security and the affirmation of individual rights—supplies its greatest lesson. For a period of time what most of the French considered the national interest took precedence over every other concern, including that for individual justice. The experience is not without parallel in our own times, when even among those devoted to securing human freedom, some have been persuaded by the threat of foreign aggression to deny, in its name, the exercise of certain basic rights.

But the Dreyfus Affair also demonstrated how a relatively small group striving to ensure justice for one individual triumphed over a majority convinced of the need to repress it. The heroic aspect of the case should not be slighted. Despite the opportunism that may have led revisionists to take political advantage of their newly found popularity, the Affair remains the prime example of a few people who gathered enough courage to withstand hostile public opinion and thus helped to preserve the institutions that could enable others to do the same. Jean Jaurès, one of the more important Dreyfusards, paid the greatest tribute when he said of them, "What matter the errors of fate and false directions of life? A few luminous and fervent hours are enough to give meaning to a lifetime."

This book introduces the topic and provides suggestions for further research. A brief overview of the Dreyfus Affair and a list of relevant presidents and prime ministers follows a timetable of events. A short survey of French history in the decades preceding the outbreak of the Affair places it in a larger historical context and sheds light on the events referred to in the next chapters. Because anti-Semitism was so significant in the Dreyfus Affair, a chapter explores its emergence in general and in France in particular. The next chapter examines the role played by labor, as spoken for by the growing numbers of Socialists, and how they were affected by events. Chapter 5 explores the ways in which historians have written about the Dreyfus Affair, from its conclusion up to the present time. Students will be led to understand how historians are very much influenced by the climate of opinion—that is, by the way people think—at the time the history is written. The concluding chapter brings to the fore the message of the ongoing battle between dueling attitudes and moralities.

Because the personalities involved played such a key part in transforming a "case" into an "affair," the biographies of the more important participants, are lengthy. Some important primary documents follow. They range from Alfred Dreyfus's diary descriptions of the torment he suffered on Devil's Island to Emile Zola's famous letter accusing the army high command and the government of conspiring to hide the truth and protect the guilty party. The photographs of newspaper illustrations and cartoons, together with portraits of the leading personalities, reveal the flavor of the inflamed passions of the day. A glossary of important terms and suggestions for further reading are designed to aid the reader. An annotated bibliography provides avenues for additional research. These suggestions include print, film, and electronic sources.

ACKNOWLEDGMENTS

I thank Linda Frey and Marsha Frey for their consistently helpful comments, suggestions, and words of encouragement. Barbara Rader provided valuable editorial help as well as guidelines. I appreciate the work of the copyeditor, Beverly Miller, who made the text cleaner and the production editor, Liz Leiba, who transformed a typescript into a book. I am especially grateful to the undergraduates on whom this material was tested. Their reactions, probably more than they realize, helped to create a better book.

CHRONOLOGY OF EVENTS

1859

October 9   Alfred Dreyfus born in Mulhouse (Alsace)

1893

January 1   Dreyfus assigned as probationer to the General Staff
                 in Paris

1894

August 15   Major Esterhazy delivers artillery mobilization plans
                 to Colonel von Schwartzkoppen, the German mili-
                 tary attaché in Paris

September 27   Arrival of the *bordereau*, the list of documents offered
                 by Esterhazy, at the Statistical Section (French Intel-
                 ligence)

October 13   The handwriting "expert," Alphonse Bertillon, names
                 Dreyfus as the writer; General Mercier calls Dreyfus
                 to the Ministry of War

October 14   Lieutenant-Colonel du Paty de Clam interrogates
                 Dreyfus

October 15   Dreyfus arrested for treason

October 31   Dreyfus identified as the officer arrested

December 19–   Secret court-martial in Paris; Dreyfus convicted and
  December 22   sentenced

1895

January 5   Dreyfus's military degradation ceremony

January	Mathieu Dreyfus, Alfred's brother, launches campaign to revise verdict and find the real culprit
End of February	Mathieu asks Bernard-Lazare to write a pamphlet defending his brother
April 13	Dreyfus arrives at Devil's Island

1896

March	Lieutenant-Colonel Picquart receives the *petit-bleu* (the special delivery letter)
August 27	Picquart informs General Boisdeffre, the chief of staff, that Esterhazy is the spy
September 3	Rumor of Dreyfus's escape, planted by Mathieu, published in London, then Paris
September 8– October 20	Dreyfus chained to his bed every night
September 14	*L'Eclair* publishes article that a secret file was used at the Dreyfus trial
September 26	Picquart sent to North Africa
November 6	Bernard-Lazare's pamphlet calling for the reopening of the Dreyfus case published in Brussels

1897

February	Jules Guérin founds the Ligue Antisémitique Français (French Anti-Semitic League)
June 29	Picquart gives his evidence to his lawyer and friend Louis Leblois
July 13-14	Leblois convinces Auguste Scheurer-Kestner, vice president of the Senate, of Dreyfus's innocence, and Scheurer-Kestner informs the Senate
November 15	Mathieu denounces Esterhazy as the spy
November 27	Emile Zola publishes his first article defending Dreyfus
December 2	Although exonerated by the army, Esterhazy demands a court-martial

1898

January 11	Esterhazy acquitted by a court-martial
January 13	Zola's "*J'accuse*" letter published in Clemenceau's newspaper; Picquart arrested
Mid- to late January	Anti-Semitic riots in provincial cities and in Algiers
January 18	Socialist deputies in Parliament proclaim neutrality in Dreyfus Affair
February 7–18	Zola trial for libel; Henry forgery cited, and Boisdeffre and generals threaten to resign
February 20	Ligue des Droits de l'Homme (League of the Rights of Man) founded
February 23	Zola, found guilty of libel, sentenced and fined
February 26	Picquart dismissed from the army
February 28	Lucie Dreyfus requests (later denied) permission to go to Devil's Island; Clemenceau-Drumont duel
July 7	Minister of War Cavaignac reads the Henry forgery to the Chamber of Deputies; Picquart denounces it as a forgery; Zola flees to England
July 27	Picquart arrested, charged with divulging secret military documents
August 10	Jaurès begins to publish *Les Preuves* (The Evidence) proving Dreyfus innocent
August 27	Esterhazy discharged from the army for "habitual misconduct"
August 30	Questioned by War Minister Cavaignac, Henry confesses his forgery; the next day he kills himself in his prison cell
August 31	General Boisdeffre resigns
September 1	Esterhazy flees France for England
September 25	Paul Déroulède revives the Ligue des Patriotes (League of Patriots); Esterhazy claims he wrote the *bordereau* on the orders of Colonel Sandherr

1899

February 10	The Chamber of Deputies requires the combined divisions of the High Court to review the Dreyfus case
February 23	Déroulède attempts a *coup*.
June 3	France's High Court anuls Dreyfus's guilty verdict and orders a new court-martial at Rennes
June 5	Zola returns to France
June 9	Dreyfus leaves Devil's Island for France; Picquart freed
June 22	Waldeck-Rousseau government of "national defense" formed
June 30-July 1	Dreyfus arrives in France and is taken to Rennes
August 7- September 9	Rennes court-martial; Dreyfus found guilty with "extenuating circumstances"
September 19	Dreyfus pardoned by President Loubet
November 17	Government proposes a general amnesty for all parties involved in the Affair, which is passed by the Chamber in December 1900

1900

January 22	The Assumptionist Order, the most belligerent of the anti-Dreyfusard Catholic congregations, is dissolved
January 28	General Mercier elected to Senate
May 28	War Minister Galliffet resigns, succeeded by General André

1901

May 1	Dreyfus publishes his memoir, *Five Years of My Life*
June 19	André presses for army reform
July 1	To curb the religious orders, an Associations Act requiring them to seek state authorization is enacted

1902

June 10	The Combes ministry, which would rigorously enforce the Associations Law and pave the way for separation of church and state, is formed
September 30	Zola dies in an accident

1903

April 6   Jaurès asks Chamber to launch investigation of the
                   "annotated *bordereau*" and hence the Rennes verdict

November 26   Dreyfus petitions for retrial

1904

March   Appeals Court begins review of Rennes verdict

July 7   Religious orders banned from all teaching

November 15   Resignation of General André

1905

July 3   Separation of church and state enacted

1906

July 12   High Court quashes Rennes verdict and declares no
                   retrial necessary

July 13   Dreyfus and Picquart reinstated into army

July 22   Dreyfus awarded Legion of Honor

October 25   Clemenceau named prime minister; appoints Piquart
                   as minister of war

1907

July 26   Dreyfus applies for retirement from army

1908

June 4   Zola's ashes sent to Panthéon, the repository of
                   France's honored dead. Attempted assassination of
                   Dreyfus

1914

January 19   Death of Picquart in an accident

August 2   Dreyfus returns to active service

September 26   Dreyfus promoted to lieutenant-colonel

1923

May 21   Death of Esterhazy in London

1935

July 11   Death of Dreyfus in Paris

1995   Dreyfus officially declared innocent by the French army

1998   The centennial of Emile Zola's "*J'accuse*"; President Jacques Chirac confirms Dreyfus's innocence.

PRESIDENTS, PRIME MINISTERS, AND MINISTERS OF WAR DURING THE DREYFUS AFFAIR

Year(s)	President	Prime Minister[1]	Minister of War
1894–1895	Casimir-Périer	Dupuy	Mercier
1895	Faure	Ribot	Mercier
1895–1896		Bourgeois	Cavaignac
1896–1898		Méline	Billot
1898		Brisson	Cavaignac
			Zurlinden
			Chanoine
1898–1899		Dupuy	Freycinet
1899	Loubet	Waldeck-Rousseau	Galliffet
			André
1902–1905		Combes	André
1905–1906		Rouvier	Berteaux
			Thomson
1906	Fallières	Sarrien	Etienne
1906–1909		Clemenceau	Picquart

1. The accurate title for the head of the government in France is president of the Council of Ministers. The more conventional "prime minister" will be used in this book.

CHAPTER 1

HISTORICAL OVERVIEW

On October 15, 1894, Alfred Dreyfus, an artillery captain attached to the French General Staff, was arrested on the charge of having betrayed his country by offering to sell military secrets to the Germans. A few weeks before, on September 26, a letter containing a list of documents, which included a description of new French artillery weapons and a field manual, had been taken from the office of the German military attaché in Paris, Colonel von Schwartzkoppen, and sent to the Statistical Section of the French War Office. The Statistical Section, created in about 1876, both employed spies and engaged in counterespionage activities. It was headed by Colonel Jean-Conrad Sandherr, an Alsatian known for his anti-Semitic views. In charge of counterespionage was then Major, soon Lieutenant-Colonel, Joseph Henry.

The letter, subsequently known as the *bordereau*, was shown to the chiefs of all the War Office departments. According to the General Staff, correct procedure was followed. A comparison of the handwriting of different officers concerned with artillery matters with that of the *bordereau* and a process of elimination convinced several officers that the culprit was Alfred Dreyfus, a trainee at the War Office, a Jew, relatively wealthy, known to be ambitious, and unpopular. On the orders of General Auguste Mercier, the minister of war, he was interrogated by staff officers, particularly by Major du Paty de Clam.

On November 1, the anti-Semitic newspaper *La Libre Parole*, edited by Edouard Drumont, announced the arrest of Dreyfus. The accused was unanimously convicted of treason by a closed court-martial on December 22. During the course of the trial, the judges had received as evidence a "secret dossier" prepared by the Statistical Section. Dreyfus was publicly degraded in a humiliating ceremony on January 5 and sentenced to penal servitude for life on Devil's Island, off the Guiana coast, the following month. On December 24, two days after his conviction, during a debate in the Chamber of Deputies (the lower house of the legislature), many speakers had expressed their indignation at the discovery of treason. Jean Jaurès, a Socialist leader who called for the death penalty, implied that the military tribunal had received secret orders to save the rich officer. Nearly all were convinced of Dreyfus's guilt, and the case seemed closed. Only the family of the condemned man, and in particular his brother, Mathieu Dreyfus, protested the decision and were determined to reverse the verdict by working to find evidence pointing to the real traitor. In this attempt, he sought the assistance of a young writer and literary critic, Bernard-Lazare.

Major Georges Picquart replaced Colonel Sandherr (who was in poor health and died in 1897) and was awarded the temporary rank of lieutenant-colonel. In March 1896 a reconstructed *petit-bleu*—a special delivery letter for use within Paris and written on thin blue paper—was taken from Schwartzkoppen's office. The letter, although never mailed, asked for "additional information" and was addressed to Major Walsin Esterhazy, a French officer with a reputation as a womanizer and dissolute spender. Picquart at first suspected him of being another traitor, but on hearing from an informer that the German War Office had never employed Dreyfus and that the only agent in German employ known to be a French officer fit the description of Esterhazy, he compared the latter's handwriting with that of the *bordereau* and was struck by the similarity. Picquart initially believed that Esterhazy and Dreyfus were accomplices, but because the handwriting on the *bordereau* was that of Esterhazy, he asked on what evidence Dreyfus had been found guilty. He raised these questions with the chief-of-staff, General Boisdeffre, on August 5, but was given no encouragement and eventually, on December 12, 1896, he was ordered to duty in North Africa.

Lieutenant-Colonel Henry, alarmed by Picquart's doubts and fully aware of the flimsy evidence used to convict Dreyfus, began to manufacture more of his own. His most important forgeries were letters from the Italian military attaché, Colonel Panizzardi, to Schwartzkoppen, designed to create the impression that Dreyfus was indeed the traitor.

Meanwhile, the brother of the accused, working independently of Picquart and assisted by Bernard-Lazare, learned of Esterhazy's guilt. Mathieu persuaded the Alsatian senator, Auguste Scheurer-Kestner, of it, and the latter asked the Senate, the upper house of the legislature, on December 7, 1897 to have the case reopened. Accordingly, and on Esterhazy's own insistence on clearing his name, a court-martial tried and found him innocent the following January 10 and 11. The Affair, which in its early stages generally had been ignored, was now creating widespread and impassioned interest, and anti-Dreyfusards hailed the acquittal as a victory. They viewed all attempts to discredit the army as necessarily being the work of a wealthy Jewish "syndicate." More interest—and passion—was aroused two days later when there appeared in Georges Clemenceau's newspaper, *L'Aurore*, an open letter by the world-renowned novelist Emile Zola to Félix Faure, president of the Republic. Zola denounced the verdict of acquittal as a "crime against humanity" and accused members of the General Staff of associating with forgers and conspirators. As a consequence of what the Socialist leader Jules Guesde called "the greatest revolutionary act of the century," more people were forced to choose between the two opposing camps of Dreyfusards and anti-Dreyfusards. Anti-Semitic riots had already broken out in provincial cities and in Algiers. Socialists, however, a newly emerging force in French politics, despite the conversion of Jaurès to the revisionist cause, refused to take a stand in what they regarded as "bourgeois wars."

The intensifying interest in the Affair took on the dimensions—at least for its most fervent partisans—of a national hysteria. Not only the popular press but commercialization of the Dreyfus Affair took place. Lithographs, posters, souvenir buttons, and cigarette boxes proliferated. Even toys and board games were designed to appeal to Dreyfusards or anti-Dreyfusards: the former could move a token around places on a board that led to rehabilitation; the latter, to execution. Sheet music, postcards, and other items (most of an anti-Dreyfusard nature) reflected a population gripped by frenzy.

In the next few months, Picquart was dismissed from the army for "professional faults," and Zola, tried and found guilty of libel (he had openly accused generals and politicians of fraud, deceit, and cover-up), was persuaded to leave France to avoid imprisonment. After the national legislative elections of May 1898, the conservative Méline ministry lost its majority in the new Chamber of Deputies, and the more liberal Henri Brisson succeeded in forming a new government. He chose as his minister of war Godefroy Cavaignac, whose reputation for integrity was unassailable. As a private citizen, Picquart sent Brisson an open letter on

July 9 in which he said that two of the letters quoted by Cavaignac, in the latter's speech two days earlier reaffirming his belief in Dreyfus's guilt, were irrelevant and the third was a forgery. Cavaignac, furious, ordered Picquart's arrest on the charge of revealing classified military documents.

On August 30 and 31, 1898, the case against Dreyfus appeared to have broken. Forced to examine the dossier, Cavaignac admitted the possibility of forgery. Henry was arrested, left a confession, and killed himself in his prison cell. Esterhazy fled to England shortly afterward and confessed in turn, but insisted that he had written the *bordereau* on the orders of his superiors. Boisdeffre and Cavaignac resigned, and the Brisson ministry began the work of revision (reopening the case). On September 29, the Criminal Chamber of France's High Court (the Court of Cassation) agreed to accept the case. The court did not have the power to find Dreyfus innocent, but it could "break" the decision of a lower court—in this case, the 1894 court-martial—and ask for another trial. Many of those who had refused to commit themselves, including Socialists, now came out for revision.

Anti-Dreyfusards, however, viewed Henry's confession and suicide as acts of courage. They accepted the version of anti-Semitic and nationalist newspapers, which insisted that only Henry's patriotic zeal had prevented him from revealing the true documents, for their disclosure implicated the kaiser (the emperor of Germany) himself, who threatened to go to war if exposed as dealing with sordid spies. *La Libre Parole* showed its esteem for the "hero" by organizing a fund for his widow. That the affair was far from over was best demonstrated by two other events. First, General Chanoine, Brisson's new minister of war, betrayed the cabinet by declaring that he shared his predecessor's opinion about Dreyfus's guilt. He said this at the reopening of Parliament, and the ministry fell. Charles Dupuy, a conservative, formed his third government. Second, Quesnay de Beaurepaire, who presided over the High Court's Civil Chamber, questioned the competency of the Court's Civil Chamber, which was to decide on the need for revision. Dreyfusards pointed out that the Criminal Chamber was noted for its liberal views and that its presiding officer was a Jew. Dupuy, however, said that he wished to give the court's verdict the force of a decree and submitted legislation to transfer the case to the court sitting as a whole. The law was voted on February 18, 1899.

The discussion of this law and its subsequent enactment definitively brought the Dreyfus Affair into the political arena. A number of

Progressists, the party of conservative republicans behind Dupuy, joined with the left, with Radicals and Socialists, in voicing their disapproval. Among those who protested was a former prime minister and now a distinguished conservative Senator, René Waldeck-Rousseau. A declaration of protest described the antirevisionist campaign, the refusal to reopen the case, as yet another assault against the French Republic, carried out by those who preferred a restoration of a monarchy or an empire.

Dreyfusards won a victory when Félix Faure, who was opposed to revision, died on February 16, and Emile Loubet, who was not opposed to revision, was elected to succeed him as president of the Republic. Another victory came June 3 when the united court broke the decision of the 1894 trial and ordered a new one. The next day, at the Auteuil racetrack, President Loubert was assaulted by an anti-Dreyfusard. On June 12, the Dupuy government, interrogated on its failure to take adequate police precautions and having lost some of its Progressist support, was overthrown. After a twelve-day crisis, René Waldeck-Rousseau, a conservative but a convinced Dreyfusard, was determined to bring closure to the affair, and managed to form a ministry of "republican defense." It included as minister of war General Gaston de Galliffet, who had played an active part in repressing the Paris Commune in 1871 (the uprising of left-wing Parisians seeking greater municipal autonomy and a continuation of the war against Prussia), and as minister of commerce Alexandre Millerand, leader of the Socialist group in the Chamber of Deputies. The cabinet, although denounced as one of "all contradictions," was approved by twenty-five votes on June 26.

On August 7, the second court-martial opened in the provincial city of Rennes, and on September 11 Dreyfus was again found guilty of treason, but by a five-to-two vote and with "extenuating circumstances." President Loubet granted him a pardon eight days later. Because of his ill health, Dreyfus accepted it. On October 10, the chamber voted against reopening the case, and at the end of the following year, it passed a law granting amnesty to all involved.

Waldeck-Rousseau, who had already taken action against the Assumptionist Fathers, the most belligerent of the anti-Dreyfusard religious orders, in 1901 submitted and obtained parliamentary approval of an Associations Act, which required the congregations to obtain authorization from Parliament. After the elections of 1902, as a result of which the Radicals became the strongest grouping in the Chamber of Deputies,

Waldeck-Rousseau resigned and was succeeded by the fiercely anticlerical Emile Combes. During the latter's tenure, religious congregations were suppressed by decree, church schools were forced to seek approval, and an attempt was made to purge the army of antirepublican officers. There soon followed separation of church and state.

On November 26, 1903, Dreyfus petitioned the High Court for revision of his case. The court accepted the petition the following March but did not quash the Rennes verdict until July 12, 1906. It fully exonerated Dreyfus and declared Esterhazy guilty of treason, but it stated that because no evidence remained to be used against Dreyfus, there would be no need for a third court-martial. On July 13, Parliament passed bills reinstating both Dreyfus and Picquart into the army. On July 22, Dreyfus was awarded the Legion of Honor. Picquart ultimately became minister of war in the government formed by Georges Clemenceau in 1906. During the preceding year, Zola's ashes had been transferred to the Panthéon, the repository of France's honored dead. Within the next few years, monuments were erected honoring Scheurer-Kestner in the Luxembourg Gardens and Waldeck-Rousseau in the Tuileries Gardens in Paris. Because the dossier on Dreyfus was destroyed in 1914, some observers remained unconvinced of his innocence. The publication of Schwartzkoppen's memoirs in 1935, which identified Esterhazy as the traitor, erased the last doubts. Not until 1995, however, would the French army officially declare Dreyfus innocent.

CHAPTER 2

BEFORE DREYFUS:
THE FRENCH POLITICAL CONTEXT

The Dreyfus Affair did not take place in political isolation. It unfolded in a Republic (the third time that the nation had experienced one) at a time when kings and emperors still ruled and so was unique by its presence. This Republic, whose existence was proclaimed in 1870 during a war with Germans (the Franco-Prussian War), came to an end in another war with them in 1940. During its seventy-year life, it endured repeated attacks from monarchists and Bonapartists on its right and from revolutionary Socialists and then Communists on its left. These attacks began long before anti-Dreyfusards condemned the Republic for permitting the defenders of a military officer convicted of treason to overturn the verdict and discredit the army, the institution relied on to preserve the nation and avenge the humiliating defeat suffered in the Franco-Prussian War.

Religious, economic, and political differences divided the French and threatened to tear the nation apart. The country was largely Catholic but possessed a strong tradition of anticlericalism. By any standard of measurement, little social legislation was enacted; working-class unhappiness with long hours, low wages, and unhealthy conditions gave rise to militant trade unions (syndicalism) and competing Socialist parties. France's democratic institutions—universal suffrage for men, many political parties reflecting every shade of political opinion, and a free press—were arguably the most progressive in the world, but they were repudiated by the critics of the regime, who yearned for the return of traditional, if authoritarian, governments. The right spark could set off a conflagration, and the Dreyfus Affair provided that spark.

The controversy surrounding Dreyfus and the opportunity it offered to anti-Republicans was not unprecedented. Numerous affairs, crises, and scandals had threatened at worst to bring down the Republic and at best to alter the social and political fabric of society. As early as 1871, when the newly created Republic sued Prussia for peace, Parisians, who had suffered severely from the Prussian siege and demanded greater municipal autonomy, rose up in civil war. The young mayor of the suburb of Montmartre, Georges Clemenceau, was indignant: he deplored the surrender and the shabby treatment accorded Parisians—for example, the end of the moratorium on the repayment of debts—by the provisional republican government. Consequently, he supported the uprising known as the Paris Commune that pitted the capital against the regime. The rebellion was repressed in bloody street fighting.

Yet Frenchmen had resented the humiliating defeat suffered at the hands of the Prussians, who took advantage of their victory to proclaim a new, united German Empire. If, as one of the republican leaders advised, they did not always speak of a war of revenge, they always thought of it. (This is why, even a quarter-century later, so many people of all political persuasions were furious on learning that a French Army officer was selling military secrets to the Germans.) Because a republican government had crushed a radical rebellion and had thus proved itself in conservative eyes, the Commune furthered the chances of securing the Republic. Because of the hostile reaction to the Commune, it ensured that the newly established Republic would be socially conservative.

It was not conservative enough for monarchists, who would accept nothing less than the restoration of a king. They would take advantage of every crisis, including the Dreyfus Affair, to bring down the Republic. Only their divisions over which king to restore and the inflexibility of the Bourbon (the old ruling family) heir to the throne, who insisted on restoring all the royal prerogatives enjoyed by his predecessors, had prevented the monarchists from reestablishing a monarchy and allowed republican institutions to develop.

The Third Republic lacked a constitution but took shape under several constitutional laws, the most important of which were voted in 1875. A bicameral legislature contained a Chamber of Deputies (the lower house), elected by all male adult citizens, and a Senate (the upper house), elected by regional legislatures. Seventy-five life senators were elected by the outgoing provisional assembly, an additional conservative check. They included the future Dreyfusard Auguste Scheurer-Kestner. Memories of

Napoleon Bonaparte and his nephew Louis Napoleon, who, in coups d'état, had transformed earlier republics into empires, still haunted republicans, who soon managed to transform the president of the Republic into little more than a figurehead.

The president of the Council of Ministers, equivalent to a prime minister, and his cabinet held real executive power. As in all other parliamentary governments, they were fully responsible to the legislature and could be ousted from office in the event that they lost the confidence of the legislature. Finally, two laws determining the mode of legislative elections completed the "constitution of 1875." Single-member constituencies relying on a run-off vote if no candidate obtained a majority on the first ballot were decided on. Because of the small size of the hundreds of electoral constituencies throughout the country, this system would allow conservative local influences to predominate, much to the detriment of future Dreyfusards. Such was the "constitution" that provided France with the longest-lived regime it had known since the coming of the Revolution of 1789.

With the election of more and more republicans, divisions among them became wider and more obvious. About a third were loosely grouped in a "radical" (that is, liberal) wing under several progressive politicians, most notably Clemenceau. They called more moderate republicans "Opportunists," a term coined to designate those who preferred to wait for an "opportune" time before voting for controversial legislation. This hesitation delayed the enactment of social reform. These Opportunists by and large formed the governments that throughout much of the 1890s refused to reopen the case against Dreyfus, even when evidence mounted that he had been unjustly condemned. However, both moderate and Radical republicans, in contrast to anti-Republican (royalist) conservatives favoring a restored monarchy, agreed that clericalism, the domination of the Catholic church in social and educational institutions, and a church that favored a restoration, was the "enemy." Anticlericalism would seal republican unity, certainly among future Dreyfusards embittered by the hostility they believed that many priests had shown to Dreyfus in particular and to Jews in general.

A constitutional crisis erupted in 1877 when a monarchist-oriented president of the Republic dissolved a republican Chamber of Deputies. The dissolution was permitted by the constitutional laws, but in view of the deputies' opposition to presidential policies, it appeared that he had acted illegally. In a bitter electoral campaign pitting republicans against monarchists, a new republican majority was returned. The president resigned and was succeeded by an avowed republican. This crisis was of enormous significance for France's Third Republic. It definitively secured the Republic, but only as a result of the defeat of anti-Republicans. Consequently, a long-standing incompatibility would endure between them and the Republic under which they had to live, an incompatibility that prevented the creation of a Tory-type conservative party (i.e., conservative but committed to the existing form of government) seeking a place within, rather than opposing, the regime itself. When many anti-Dreyfusards would condemn the Republic for allowing the army to be criticized by Dreyfus's supporters, they were reflecting a long-standing tradition in French political life.

Of equal significance was the loss suffered in presidential authority. Never again would the Republic's president try to dissolve the Chamber of Deputies. With the disuse of this check on its power, the legislature was to become all-powerful and make life for future governments increasingly unstable. Even without the turbulence left in the wake of the Dreyfus Affair, governments in France seldom survived more than a year in office. The reluctance of subsequent presidents to call on strong personalities to serve as prime minister (they feared a strong prime minister might carry out a coup in the manner of the Bonapartes) also did much to prevent the establishment of a strong and stable government. This ministerial instability (that is, short-lived governments) thus caused the constitutional development of France to follow a path different from that of Great Britain or the United States. Legislative domination, a multiplicity of parties with those at the opposite ends of the political spectrum (monarchists and revolutionary socialists) opposed to the regime itself, and the refusal to ask powerful personalities to form governments help to explain the short-lived tenures of French governments. Not until 1899, when a government of "republican defense" was established to put an end to the Affair, would one last as long as three years.

In the 1880s, an exception to a long line of weak prime ministers emerged: a strong personality managed to form cabinets on two occasions. Jules Ferry was a cold and austere Opportunist. Like his predecessors, he never tired of reminding liberal urban populations how insecure the Republic was and how nothing must disturb and possibly alienate the vast body of public opinion that still existed in the countryside and on whose tolerance the regime had been established. He warned that the small farmers, who constituted a majority of the population, would not support the taxes required to fund expensive social programs. He realistically sought only legislation that he knew could be enacted. Ferry emphasized issues on which all republicans could agree, such as removing primary education from church control by making it compulsory and secular, and he pursued this policy aggressively. This legislation was prompted by patriotic and social as well as by anticlerical and political motives. The pedagogical —and patriotic—supremacy of Prussian schoolmasters had been seen as an indirect cause of France's defeat in 1870–1871, and few republicans denied that a free and compulsory primary education would provide greater equality of opportunity—and more support for the Republic. It was Ferry's colonial policy, which established a protectorate in Tunisia and secured Indochina for France, that aroused Radical as well as monarchist opposition. Both left and right argued that French treasure and energy expended abroad would make France more vulnerable at home and delay the long-anticipated war of revenge against Germany. They joined forces to overthrow the Ferry government in a parliamentary vote of no confidence in 1884 and in so doing demonstrated that a strong feeling of nationalism, and specifically resentment of Germany, drove French public opinion.

The great crisis that threatened the Republic in the late 1880s arose from the immense popularity—and fears generated by that popularity— of an army general turned politician, Georges Boulanger. He had shown concern for the well-being of his troops and, most important, called himself an avowed republican. Since their exclusion from administrative careers in 1879, monarchists had made the army something of a stronghold, and hopes of democratizing it had led Radicals to advance Boulanger's candidacy. His career had been remarkable. A lieutenant-colonel at age thirty-three, four campaigns, six wounds, and the Legion of Honor by age thirty-five, he reached the rank of general at age forty-three. On Clemenceau's recommendation, he was named minister of war. An apparently successful encounter with the German chancellor Bismarck over the hasty incarceration of a French national and a series of popular orders increased his already prodigious renown. In a by-election in the Seine Department (Paris and its environs), the general's supporters

submitted his name; although he was on active duty and therefore ineli-
gible, he nevertheless easily amassed over 100,000 votes. Opportunist and
conservative deputies, however, resented his disdainful attitude toward the
legislature and feared possible dictatorial aspirations. When "exiled" to
command the Thirteenth Army Corps in a distant provincial town, Paul
Déroulède, president of the nationalist League of Patriots, called Boulanger
"the only man who makes Germany afraid." The huge and noisy demon-
stration at the railway station from which he was to depart—his frenzied
supporters lay down on the tracks to prevent his leaving—finally convinced most Radicals, including Clemenceau, that their continued support
might prove disastrous for the Republic.

Deserted by his former Radical sponsors yet unwilling to resign himself to obscurity, Boulanger visited and received support from the prince-
imperial, the descendant of the Bonapartists, in Switzerland and members
of the nobility, including perhaps the duke of Orléans, the royalist claim-
ant to the throne. It would be a mistake, however, to see Boulangism as a
movement supported only by conservatives. It obtained much of its popular, if not its financial, backing from the left. Like the Dreyfus Affair, of
which in a number of ways it was a precursor, Boulangism was a movement uniting all the opponents of the republican regime, and Boulanger
probably benefited from events more than he directed them. Economic
depression, political agitation for constitutional revision, and the reaction
to German threats of war all helped to create an environment favorable
to the rise of a hero.

Boulanger became an eligible candidate when he resigned from the
army. His backers, ranging from assorted Socialists to royalists, offered a
vague program with something for everyone. In the spring and summer
of 1888, he was elected to the Chamber in several departments. The following January, in the Seine Department, he won an 80,000-vote majority
against the candidate of the combined republican opposition. As it would
again ten years later, during the height of the Dreyfus Affair, Paris had gone
nationalist; Boulanger was acclaimed on the boulevards, and a coup
seemed imminent. But for reasons still not clear, he either refused or hesitated too long to take power, and the staggered republicans began to pull
themselves together. The government dissolved the League of Patriots (to
be revived by Déroulède during the Dreyfus Affair) and daringly charged
Boulanger with violating national security. To the stupefaction of his sup-

porters, he fled to Brussels. He was condemned in absentia and two years later killed himself on the grave of the mistress he said he had left France to join.

Boulangists suffered a crushing defeat in the elections of 1889. Only about forty were sent to the Chamber, and the Republic appeared to have emerged strengthened by its ordeal. But the causes and consequences of Boulangism were to endure. For one, the long-standing Radical campaign for constitutional revision, for elimination of the presidency and the Senate, was thoroughly discredited after the use made of it by Boulanger. Aside from changes in the electoral system, the constitutional laws of 1875 would generally hold throughout the Third Republic (and for that matter, the Fourth Republic, which succeeded it after World War II). Furthermore, in allying themselves with the losing side, conservatives lost, at least for a decade, any chance of bringing down the regime. They would have to wait until the passions reawakened by the Dreyfus Affair provided another opportunity. In waging early and successful war against Boulangism, Opportunists appeared to have gained the most, and in fact they dominated nearly every government until 1899.

Opportunist successes, however, seemed a poor choice for one product of expanding industrialization: the steadily rising number of workers, who began to turn to newer and more radical means of political expression. The coming decade would see the emergence of an energetic, if disunited, Socialist movement in France. As a final result of the Boulangist craze, the proven ability of republicans to join in combating antirepublicans and clerical forces, and their reluctance to distinguish between the two, brought about an attempt to rally Catholics to the Republic.

By 1890, the Republic had lasted longer than any other regime since Louis XV's in the early eighteenth century, and it appeared capable of enjoying a long life to come. The realistic and clear-sighted Pope Leo XIII, unhappy with the poor reception accorded his predecessor, recognized that by continuing their intransigent opposition to the Republic, Catholics would hurt nobody but themselves. It seemed useless to tie the Church to a losing conservative (anti-Republican) cause. On the other hand, Opportunists—or Progressists, as they now began to call themselves— could not enact further anticlerical legislation without abrogating the Concordat of 1801–1802, which had made religious establishments state agencies and provided salaries for priests. Unlike Radicals, they refused to consider separation of church and state. By getting the Church to abandon the monarchy and play a neutral role in politics, the pope hoped to disarm republican adversaries of the Church in France. However, this movement to bring Catholics to the support of the Republic, known as the *Ralliement* (rallying), faced stubborn resistance. Most royalist deputies rejected the pope's attempt to reshape their nonreligious (political) conduct, while Radicals and Socialists saw papal policy as a clever maneuver designed to increase its political influence. In the election of 1893, only thirty-five *ralliés* were successful, and during the Dreyfus Affair, some religious orders and a significant number of priests came over to the anti-Dreyfusard, and even anti-Republican, cause.

Parliamentary institutions were once more discredited by, and ex-Boulangists sought revenge in, the events connected with the Panama Affair. A French company represented by Ferdinand de Lesseps, the engineer who had built the Suez Canal, was organized to dig a canal through the Isthmus of Panama. Its backers were overly optimistic, neglected to take thorough sanitation measures, and used poor equipment, and delay followed delay. In the early 1890s, the company received successive loans from a sympathetic Parliament—even the right to issue shares in a public lottery. When the lottery failed, the enterprise itself collapsed. Some important financiers—including a relation of a future Dreyfusard chief, Joseph Reinach—and leading politicians—including an unjustly implicated Georges Clemenceau—found themselves involved in a sordid scandal: together with some important Paris newspaper editors, charged with having accepted bribes to solicit support for the lottery.

The country accused itself of social decay and demanded that the "thieves" be thrown out of office. The Panama Affair was exploited by enemies of the regime in hopes of discrediting it, and a disgusted public replaced a large number of deputies seeking reelection with younger men. Socialists seized the opportunity to denounce capitalist corruption. The Panama Affair had much to do with sending between forty and fifty socialist candidates to the Chamber in the legislative elections of 1893, making the movement a force to be reckoned with. In that election, only seventy-eight royalists and Boulangists were successful, as compared to over five hundred republicans. The Progressists, remained ascendant, but signs of dissatisfaction were growing, particularly from those who felt themselves disadvantaged as French society grew more industrialized and urban.

The complicated and strife-ridden history of socialism in France, a movement whose leaders played an important part in the Dreyfus Affair, offers several examples of dissent erupting into schism. The discordant and opposed factions of which the movement was composed did not unite until after the turn of the century. Only six avowed Socialists had sat in the 1885–1889 Chamber, but a strike and brutal murder at the mining town of Decazeville in 1886 momentarily turned attention to social issues and led to the formation of a workers' group of deputies. The participation in these debates of young Radicals like Alexandre Millerand and Jean Jaurès, sympathetic to social reform and soon to convert to the Socialist cause, had aroused speculation about a parliamentary Socialist party. As major Socialist spokesmen, both men would initially urge labor to take no part in the Dreyfusard struggle, but ultimately they would come to the defense of the accused officer. Jaurès, in particular, would bring his followers to the support of both Dreyfus and the Republic.

French socialism had many roots, but the movement, during its recovery from the reprisals taken after the Paris Commune, was characterized by the expansion of revolutionary Marxism, in part because of the persistent efforts of such propagandists and organizers as the journalist and organizer Jules Guesde and Karl Marx's son-in-law, Paul Lafargue. However, the poor showing of revolutionary Marxists in the 1881 elections helped to generate a "reformist" reaction within the party. Resentment was expressed toward Marx and German ideas, and conversely, emphasis placed on French tradition and needs, and on reform, rather than revolution as the proper vehicle to achieve Socialist goals. Reformists and revolutionaries, and the various splinter groups among them, formed separate factions within the Socialist movement. Moreover, a group of "independent" Socialists, rejecting affiliation to any faction as being too doctrinaire, denying that existing social phenomena derived from economic causes alone, and advocating a newer, and more integral form of socialism (one that focused on psychological as well as material concerns), emerged in the early 1890s. This group proposed to transform society not only economically but also philosophically and morally, and was found most attractive by such newcomers as Millerand and Jaurès. These "Independents" called for immediate reforms and sought to unite Socialists in an evolutionary (in contrast to a revolutionary), nonviolent approach. They would give French Socialism its first journal, many of its first deputies, and ultimately, as part of the effort to wind down the Dreyfus Affair, its first member of a government.

As the century drew to a close, more Socialists appeared reconciled to a reformist policy. Nearly all approved of Millerand's important 1896 speech defending that policy, and of those who objected, most found it too doctrinaire, not too flexible. Many French Socialists supported the alliance made with Czarist Russia, considered the most reactionary regime in Europe, and supported as well an all-Radical cabinet in 1896. Progressists then returned to power with a government headed by the politician who earlier had pushed through tariff legislation, Jules Méline. They would remain there until the upheaval of the Dreyfus Affair split their party and brought the Radicals, again supported by the Socialists, back to power.

In view of the significant victory won by republicans in the election of 1893, and especially of the increased representation of Radical and Socialist candidates, it is no longer accurate to consider the Dreyfus Affair as a great turning point in the history of France's Third Republic. The ultimate success of the Dreyfusards, however, brought an even greater Radical victory, and with Socialist support in the Chamber, it was usually Radical ministries that governed the nation until World War I. The beginning of some attempts to enact social legislation, as well as the culmination of anticlerical legislation in the separation of church and state, characterize the period. All this was made possible by the Dreyfus Affair.

CHAPTER 3

ANTI-SEMITISM AND THE DREYFUS AFFAIR

Anti-Semitism is commonly taken to mean hostility or prejudice against Jews and it can range from strong dislike to violent hatred. Most psychologists and social scientists view anti-Semitism as an irrational form of behavior based on the need for a scapegoat to justify aggression or relieve guilt. Before the nineteenth century, anti-Semitism was largely religious in nature, having first emerged in the second half of the first millennium B.C.E. (Before the Common Era) and later reinforced by the enmity shown Jews by the Christian church. Animosity developed in late antiquity because monotheism—the uncompromising belief in one God—discouraged Jews from recognizing or respecting Greek or Roman deities. In addition, their retention of practices such as circumcision, dietary regulations, and cleanliness laws set Jews apart and made assimilation difficult. The Greco-Roman world was hostile to Judaism, and this hostility encouraged the growth of such myths as human sacrifice in the Temple.

With the coming of Christianity, dislike of the Jews hardened into persecution, expulsion, geographical restriction, and legends. Jews were accused of the crucifixion of Jesus Christ. At the end of the fifteenth century Jews unwilling to convert to Catholicism or those who had converted but were suspected of maintaining Jewish practices, were forced to leave Spain. Elsewhere Jews were forbidden to own land and so forced into limited commercial activities, such as the money-lending, which was prohibited to Christians as usury. Jews were permitted to live only in certain regions or, within cities, restricted areas (ghettos). Wild false stories circulated of ritual murder of Christian children committed by Jews. (Not until the 1960s, when the Second Vatican Council was convened, would the Catholic Church officially repudiate its accusation that the Jews were responsible for Christ's death and finally condemn anti-Semitic thought.)

Because of the absolute distinction they drew between God and man, the very essence of their faith, Jews rejected the divinity of Jesus. To Christians, this rejection—and the continued survival of the Jews as a distinct group—was seen as a perpetual insult, and Church fathers such as Augustine believed that the Jews' loss of their homeland served as divine retribution. The continued refusal of Jews to assimilate, to lose themselves in the midst of the people now surrounding them, strengthened the ideology of a Christian anti-Judaism that both encouraged and rationalized discrimination and even physical attacks. These were sanctioned by such medieval popes as Gregory the Great (590–604). They took the form of massacres or forced conversions, such as those in German-speaking Mainz and English-speaking York in the eleventh century. A decree of Pope Innocent III in 1215 required Jews to wear badges identifying them as such. Crusaders targeted Jews as well as Muslims in the thirteenth century and blamed Jews for the Black Death, the plague that ravaged Europe in the fourteenth century.

The emancipation of the Jews in the wake of the French Revolution, initially continued by Napoleon in areas under French rule, lifted civil restrictions, granted Jews equal rights under the law, and so promoted assimilation. "Let there be neither Jews nor Christians except at the hour of prayer for those who pray," proclaimed an assimilated Jew celebrating the centennial of the Revolution. A rabbi, voicing appreciation to the country "which has so generously adopted us," proudly declared that "thanks to God, there are no longer but Frenchmen in France." The Grand Rabbi of Paris at his installation in 1891 spoke of the links between "the French genius" and "the fundamental spirit of Judaism" and described the French as "this elect people of modern times."[1] French Jews thought of themselves as French citizens who practiced Judaism as their religion. Similarly, numerous German Jews considered themselves Germans, English Jews English, etc. (Emancipation triggered a variant of Judaism known in Europe as "Liberal"—later, in the United States, as "Reform," in which assimilated Jews held services in the language of their country as well as in Hebrew. Those who retained Hebrew and kept traditional religious and dietary practices were known as "Orthodox.") But if for many Jews, Judaism was now a purely religious denomination, anti-Jewish prejudice did not end. Many Gentiles (non-Jews) and much of their clergy castigated Jews as a people of "deicide" (the act of killing a god). To combat prejudice and discrimination, the Alliance Israélite Universelle was established in 1860 in France.

In the late nineteenth century the "Jewish Question" became increasingly complicated with the development of pseudoscientific theories of race, and the resulting merger of nationalism and racism strengthened anti-Jewish sentiment. German scholars exploring the origins of language were the first to distinguish between the Aryan or Indo-European peoples, with their roots in Sanskrit, and the Semitic peoples, with roots in the Hebraic language groups. The French popularized these ideas. Joseph Gobineau and, later, an Englishman-turned-German, Houston Stewart Chamberlain promulgated racial theories that proclaimed Aryans superior and Semitic peoples inferior. Their ideas rekindled anti-Jewish sentiment on the part of the French writer Maurice Barrès, the German composer Richard Wagner, and others.

Religious and then economic resentments thus gave way to racial prejudice, which overlay hostility to Jews with a modern and scientific veneer; anti-Judaism now became anti-Semitism. And if Jews now constituted a "race" (a patently absurd notion given the variety of racial backgrounds of those who identified themselves as Jews and one repudiated by anthropologists), then conversion no longer served as an option for racists seeking a solution to the Jewish "problem." In countries as diverse as Czarist Russia, imperial Germany and Austria, and democratic France, where Christian influence blended with political conservatism and economic depression threatened the livelihood of many, anti-Semitism emerged as a popular political movement. (It was in Germany in 1879 that the term *anti-Semitism*, was introduced into the political vocabulary by Hamburg pamphleteer Wilhelm Marr. His resentment of the arrival of masses of *Östjuden*—Eastern European Jews fleeing persecution in Russia and Russian Poland—led him to found the Anti-Semitic League.)

Still, for a century before the Dreyfus Affair, French Jews had been among the most successfully assimilated Jews in Western Europe. Such Jews as the philosopher Henri Bergson, the sociologist Emile Durkheim, and the young theater critic Léon Blum were distinguishing themselves in their respective fields of expertise. They were doing so as Jews, without converting to Christianity. Most French Jews blended into the local religious landscape. Some Reform rabbis considered holding Sabbath services on Sundays, and other ceremonies for children resembled baptisms and First Communions. Flowers on coffins, collection plates, rabbinical visits to bedsides of the dying, singing in synagogue, organ music, and sermons were all modeled on Christian practice. It was estimated that there were only 500 true Orthodox Jews in the entire country. Assimilation thus seemed to have succeeded in France.[2] This helps to explain why at the time of Dreyfus's arrest, Jewish leaders—who had no reason to doubt the army's judgment—were appalled by his alleged crime and tried to play things down to avoid an anti-Semitic backlash. When Dreyfus was deported to Devil's Island, they accepted the decision and felt ashamed of his guilt.

Anti-Semitism in France—and in the rest of Western Europe—was influenced by anti-Semitism in Russia, where the persecution of Jews was virulent and systematic. Jews were confined to a "Pale of Settlement," the twenty-five western-most provinces reaching from the Baltic to the Black Sea, and subject to a twenty-five-year military conscription. Admittedly, the inefficiency of the authorities, the possibility of bribery, and the lack of consistent enforcement made life bearable, if difficult, for Jews.

Conditions worsened in the 1870s when the assassination of Czar Alexander II unleashed a wave of repression against Jews. Although not responsible for the assassination, they were viewed as outsiders hostile to the regime and the Russian Orthodox Church. The state now sanctioned *pogroms* (the Russian word for devastation), local police-organized Jew hunts accompanied by pillage, rape, and destruction of property. In the nineteenth century, Russia (including Russian-occupied Poland) was the only country where anti-Semitism was official state policy. By the early years of the twentieth century, the goal of reducing the Jewish population received ideological cover with the publication of a state-sanctioned forgery—the so-called "Protocols of the Elders of Zion." Written in France in the 1890s by an anonymous author in the service of the Russian police to justify the regime's anti-Semitic statutes, it described an alleged conspiracy of Jewish leaders to subvert existing political and economic institutions. In a fantastic scenario, these "elders" were supposed to have met in a Prague cemetery where they plotted to take over the world on behalf of international Jewry. The "Protocols" were published in 1903 and subsequently circulated throughout the world.

Although a handful of Russian and Polish Jews driven by persecution stayed to support revolutionary movements, millions chose to emigrate to Western Europe and the United States. It was this wave of immigrants, many distinguished by their Orthodox garb and their inability to speak any language other than Yiddish (a mixture of Hebrew and medieval German), that western Europeans found so economically and socially threatening. All evils could be blamed with impunity on them; their unpopularity was exploited by demagogues, such as Edouard Drumont in France, to stir the masses against the existing government and find an outlet for popular discontent.

Certainly part of the explanation for mounting intolerance in France in the 1880s came from the perceived "invasion" of Jews fleeing the East and disproportionately settling in Paris. In 1840, only about 70,000 Jews lived in France, most in the eastern regions of Alsace and Lorraine. The arrival of masses—120,000 over the course of a generation—of German, Russian, and Polish Jews, impoverished, different in appearance and speech, generated distrust and hostility. Although by choosing France they had given the clearest indication of where their loyalty was placed, many who lived there, including the Dreyfus family, relocated. When France ceded Alsace to the German Empire after the Franco-Prussian War of 1870–1871, they nevertheless, were viewed as Germans. Edouard Drumont wrote in *La France Juive*, published in 1886, that France was being "colonized" by Jews, whom he claimed then numbered half a million. In fact, according to the census of 1890, there were fewer than 68,000 Jews in mainland France (50,000 in Paris) and another 43,000 in Algeria, under French control. The total population of France was then approaching 39 million, so the Jewish community in France itself amounted to less than 0.2 percent of the population.

The vast majority of French Jews were not overly religious. Living in perhaps the most liberal and democratic regime in Europe, they identified themselves as French and believed they had found safety in France's Third Republic, which constitutionally embodied these values. They regarded themselves as patriots.

For many historians, the manifestations of anti-Semitism in France unleashed by Jewish immigration are best explained in terms of social and economic changes in France during the last quarter of the nineteenth century. Modernization, industrialization (although perhaps slower in France than in Germany or the United States), urbanization, and the growth and concentration of business and financial establishments brought about dislocation and economic resentment. Democratic forms, the parliamentary system of government, and the Republic itself raised related and equivalent fears in the political sector. The secularism that accompanied these changes was perceived as a threat against traditional religious belief and particularly against the Catholic church.[3] Anti-Semitism became a major weapon employed by opponents of liberalism and the republican state, and it consequently took on a political dimension. It was because Dreyfus was a Jew who had risen to the highest ranks in the army that the attacks against him escalated into a full-fledged assault against the Republic itself and all that it stood for—most significant, equality under the law and careers open to talent regardless of birth or social status. (The juncture of anti-Semitism and anti-Republicanism would resurface in twentieth-century France, most notably in the Vichy government that collaborated with Germany during World War II and in the bitter campaigns waged against two Jewish prime ministers: Léon Blum in 1937 and 1938 and Pierre Mendès-France in 1954–1955.)[4]

The influx of Jews and the anxieties created by a more urban and secular society found expression in greater irrationalism, that is, an emphasis on instinct and a corresponding distrust of critical intelligence. A cultural revolt and a movement toward a new consciousness challenged the liberal values that had emerged from the eighteenth century's emphasis on reason and reinforced by the scientific and technological achievements associated with nineteenth-century progress. A vague ideology emerged near the end of the nineteenth century that condemned alike the "uprooted intellectual," the "wandering Jew," and the "international capitalist," all considered detestable and embodiments of a decadent, corrupt, and materialistic society. These confused but vigorous ideas strengthened latent anti-Semitic sentiments.

For those who saw conspiracy—plots to subvert the existing social order—at work, the Jew, and to a lesser extent the Protestant and the Freemason, had necessarily organized and inspired the decadence of the times. Lacking a homeland, the Jew was viewed as the eternal wanderer. Lacking land of his own, he was a merchant. The stereotype of the Jew as a rootless, greedy businessman was reinforced in France by the renown of a few great banking families, chiefly the Rothschilds and Pereires. The novelist Maurice Barrès was to write, "That Dreyfus is capable of treason I deduce from his race."[5] Although Jews could be found in business and the professions, nevertheless, most were ordinary workers, and about 40 percent of those residing in Paris were poor.

The 1882 collapse of a Catholic banking establishment, the Union Générale, helped to crystallize the formation of a modern anti-Semitic ideology. The bank had been established four years earlier to provide Catholics with an alternative to banking houses thought to be owned by Jewish and Protestant interests. Church institutions and Catholic families, as well as thousands of small investors, deposited funds. Although mismanagement accounted for the bank's failure, the Catholic press and then mass-circulation dailies created fictionalized accounts of Jewish bankers, especially the Rothschilds, who had caused its fall. Anti-Semites increasingly became obsessed with the role Jews allegedly played in finance capitalism. The Assumptionist religious order led the campaign. Selected and supported by the papacy to "re-Christianize France" by organizing mass pilgrimages to Rome and "new miracle centers" such as Lourdes, the order, founded in 1847, was the first to bring modern methods to religious revivalism. The fathers, for example, hired special trains to assemble vast crowds, and they founded a successful publishing house and a mass circulation daily, *La Croix*. They contended that the collapse of the Union Générale was the work of a Jewish, Protestant, and Freemason conspiracy and pledged that *La Croix* would combat "the trio of hate."[6] When the Panama Canal scandal broke ten years later—specifically the attempts of its promoters to bribe legislators in order to secure state funding for the project—the role of Jewish financiers was grossly exaggerated in the popular press and fueled anti-Semitic myths about Jewish financial domination.

The mobilizing power and revolutionary force of anti-Semitism became apparent in Boulangism, the nationalist and authoritarian movement that centered on a popular general in the late 1880s and gave birth to a politically based anti-Semitism.[7] Boulanger himself was not anti-Semitic, a failing for which he was reproached by such supporters as Barrès and the intensely nationalistic Paul Déroulède. But as Boulangism became an organized movement independent from its nominal leader, anti-Semitism became increasingly embedded within it, from its top executives down to its rank and file. Insofar as the movement drew support from the working class, the portrayal of the Jew as dominating the country's economic life provided a ready explanation for the misery experienced by common workers. Anti-Semites claimed that in Algeria, the "vile Yids" had organized a vast currency speculation, and in eastern France, Jewish moneylenders and merchants were sowing economic ruin. The claim was always the same: regions were reduced to poverty by small groups of Jewish merchants and usurers. Accordingly, public opinion was mobilized on behalf of the movement in considerable degree because of the ability of its propagandists to exploit anti-Semitic themes.

The Union Générale collapse, the Panama Canal scandal, economic depression, resentment of the German victory in 1871, and Jewish immigration thus combined to shape the climate exploited by Drumont, who in historian Michael Marrus's words became "the most outstanding purveyor of anti-Semitism in French history."[8] When his La France juive appeared in 1886, it found an audience ready for his message. The book sold better than any other political work in the century, going through two hundred printings, and when it was serialized in a popular newspaper, it was even more widely read. Other anti-Semitic works appeared that also held the Jews responsible for all of France's problems. According to Robert Byrnes, a historian of French anti-Semitism, literature attacking the Jews rose from an annual average of less than one publication from 1879 through 1885 to twenty in 1889.[9] In 1892 the newspaper La Libre Parole launched its campaign against Jews in the army, calling them potential traitors, and La Croix, joined vigorously in the attack. La Croix called itself in 1890 "the most anti-Jewish newspaper in France, the one that bears Christ, the sign of horror for all Jews."[10] Small wonder then, that the notoriously anti-Semitic Colonel Sandherr, on hearing that Dreyfus was a possible suspect slapped his forehead and exclaimed, "I should have known." The fact that earlier in 1894 France had signed a military alliance with Russia made the Jews all the more suspect: they were known for hating the Tsarist regime.

Drumont's writings raised "the myths associated with Judaism to the level of ideology and political involvement."[11] His message of hate reached out to workers and the small bourgeoisie, whose economic plight he blamed on Jewish financiers and cosmopolitan Socialists, who, he insisted, were all Jews from Karl Marx on. He thus blended anti-Semitism with a vulgar populism that blamed a minority of Jewish profiteers for the economic misfortunes of the rest of the French populace.

Anti-Jewish political movements seeking to take advantage of growing anti-Semitic sentiment now began to spring up. The *Ligue nationale antisémitique* (National Anti-Semitic League) was founded by Drumont and others in 1889, and many of its members joined in support of the popular General Boulanger. Specifically excluded from membership were Jews and criminals (except those convicted in courts presided over by Jews); it aimed at fighting the "pernicious influence of the financial sway of the Jews whose clandestine and merciless conspiracy jeopardizes the welfare, honor, and security of France daily."[12] In 1897, Jules Guérin, a disciple of Drumont, founded the *Ligue Antisémitique Française* (the French Anti-Semitic League), which recruited between 5,000 and 10,000 members. It was oriented toward the political left: many of its adherents regarded themselves as "socialists," who fulminated against big capital and big finance. At the end of 1898, Paul Déroulède revived his *Ligue des Patriotes* (League of Patriots), which although republican was amenable to the anti-Semitism of Guérin. Yet another extraparliamentary group was the *Ligue de la Patrie Française* (League of the French Fatherland). Founded in January 1899 by school teachers and claiming 40,000 adherents, it enlisted the support of such intellectuals as the literary critic Jules Lemaître to show that Dreyfusards did not have a monopoly of intellectuals. Seen as too patrician and abstract, younger men inclined to extremism and action founded their own review, the *Action Française* and, taking the name of the journal in July 1899, broke away from the parent organization. It soon came under the influence of the journalist Charles Maurras, who saw the salvation of France in the restoration of the monarchy. The impassioned events of the Dreyfus Affair, and in particular Zola's revolutionary accusations and the response they engendered, completed the process of politicizing anti-Semitic sentiment. In 1898, anti-Semitic riots and demonstrations broke out in nearly seventy towns and cities in France, requiring the presence of troops on at least five occasions. That same year, twenty-two openly anti-Semitic members of Parliament were elected, and forty more would support anti-Semitic legislation.[13]

Most historians now deny the existence of an anti-Semitic plot—although not widespread anti-Semitic feelings—on the part of the army against the unfortunate captain. (Only Major Henry, who actually forged evidence, in contrast to the cowardice and stupidity of his colleagues, acted in bad faith.) It was the anti-Semitic press, *La Libre Parole* and *La Croix,* that whipped up anti-Jewish sentiment when it broke the story of a Jewish officer's arrest and proclaimed that "all Jewry" was behind the "traitor." The street riots and demonstrations that reached even into the austere lecture halls of the Sorbonne were fueled by anti-Semitic rage against attempts to reopen the trial.

Paradoxically, thanks to the extremists in the Dreyfusard camp whose anticlerical ferocity and desire to take vengeance on the church as well as anti-Dreyfusard efforts to keep the unfortunate victim on Devil's Island, the Affair succeeded in institutionalizing anti-Semitism. Maurras's league evolved into a pro-fascist, anti-Semitic movement. It formed the most vicious element in the Vichy regime, which collaborated with Nazi Germany between 1940 and 1944 and helped to send between 75,000 and 77,000 Jews, native born and refugee, to their deaths. Vichy's Statute of October 3, 1940, prohibited Jews, defined on religious and racial grounds, from all political, juridical, and civil service positions, including education and the armed forces. These and other acts corresponded with the demands of French anti-Semites during and after the Dreyfus Affair and, as Robert Paxton and Michael Marrus have shown, were not the product of German pressure.[14] Although in the Dreyfus Affair no conspiracy, certainly no Jewish conspiracy, had ever existed, the Dreyfusard victory convinced many Frenchmen that there indeed had been one. Maurras was not alone in seeing Vichy as "belated revenge."[15] Clearly, if the heated passions of the Dreyfus Affair cooled in the decade before World War I, the negative stereotype of the Jew persisted. But in French history, no regime other than Vichy, whether republican, royalist, or Bonapartist, ever repudiated the Jewish emancipation passed into law during the eighteenth-century Revolution.[16] Without denying the effects of deeply rooted prejudice, it is more useful to regard an outbreak of anti-Semitism, whether manifested in the Dreyfus Affair or at any other time, less as an inbred psychological or political reflex and more as the product of a particular historical context.

Notes

1. Cited in Jean-Denis Bredin, *The Affair: The Case of Alfred Dreyfus* (New York: George Braziller, 1986), 24; Paula Hyman, *From Dreyfus to Vichy: The Remaking of French Jewry, 1906–1939* (New York: Columbia University Press, 1979), 7; Paul Johnson, *A History of the Jews* (New York: Harper, 1988), 381.

2. Hyman, 1; Johnson, 381.

3. Examples of such historians are Pierre Birnbaum, Michel Winock, Stephen Wilson, Jean-Denis Bredin, Zeev Sternshell, Michael Marrus, and Robert Paxton. See the discussion in Vicki Caron, "The 'Jewish question' from Dreyfus to Vichy" in Martin S. Alexander, ed., *French History since Napoleon* (New York: Oxford University Press, 1999), 173–181.

4. Alexander, 174.

5. Cited in Bredin, 28.

6. Robert Hoffman, *More Than a Trial: The Struggle over Captain Dreyfus.* (New York: Free Press, 1980), 82; Johnson, 385.

7. The thesis of Zeev Sternhell, "The Roots of Popular Anti-Semitism in the Third Republic," in Frances Malino and Bernard Wasserstein, eds., *The Jews in Modern France* (Hanover, N.H.: University Press of New England, 1985), 104.

8. Michael Marrus, "Popular Anti-Semitism," in Norman Kleeblatt, ed., *The Dreyfus Affair: Art, Truth, and Justice* (Berkeley and London: University of California Press, 1987), 52; see the discussion of Drumont in the Biographies section.

9. Cited by Marrus, 54.

10. Bredin, 29.

11. Michel Winnock, "Edouard Drumont et l'antisémitisme en France avant l'Affaire Dreyfus," *Esprit* (May 1971): 1097–1099.

12. Wilhelm Herzog, *From Dreyfus to Pétain: The Struggle of a Republic* (New York: Creative Age Press, 1947), 31–32.

13. Stephen Wilson, *Ideology and Experience: Antisemitism in France at the Time of the Dreyfus Affair* (Rutherford, N.J.: Fairleigh Dickinson University Press, 1982), 734.

14. Robert Paxton and Michael Marrus, *Vichy France and the Jews* (New York: Basic Books, 1991). That a majority of the 330,000 Jews in France survived is largely explained by the willingness of many within the French population to shelter them.

15. Johnson, 390. The thesis of Herzog's *From Dreyfus to Pétain*.

16. Caron, 175–176.

CHAPTER 4

SOCIALISTS AND THE DREYFUS AFFAIR

The Dreyfus Affair profoundly affected the history of socialism in France—and for that matter, outside France. It made possible for the first time the entry of a Socialist, Alexandre Millerand, into a regularly established bourgeois or non-Socialist government. It pitted parliamentary reformist Socialists against Socialists still committed to revolutionary strategies—the future Communists. Perhaps most important and thanks in large measure to Jean Jaurès, the Socialist party's greatest orator and leading voice for a more humanistic, more "integral" socialism, it brought Socialists and much of their labor constituency to the support of the Republic. At first, however, it was not Jaurès's view—that Socialists must come to the defense of the rich officer—that prevailed. It was that of the post-1898 leader of the parliamentary Socialists, Millerand, who urged his colleagues not to take sides in the Dreyfus Affair.

Millerand first took a neutral position toward Dreyfus and showed concern only about political and legal considerations. In December 1897, to the applause of the extreme left in the Chamber of Deputies, he insisted that the government cease equivocating and reply firmly to Dreyfusard demands for revision. But the Socialist spokesman was taking advantage of the opportunity to attack Prime Minister Méline and was neither condemning nor defending Dreyfus. He rejected Méline's explanation that the question was strictly one of law and not the concern of the government or of parliament, neither of which, according to the prime minister, was to question the rendered judgment (*la chose jugée*). The government held that questioning juridical decisions repudiated French tradition, and Méline's stand was endorsed by General Billot, the minister of war, who swore that Dreyfus had been justly sentenced. Avoiding the issue, replied Millerand, would not stop Dreyfusards from striving to reopen the case, and in such a serious matter the government had to take a stand. The Chamber nevertheless passed a resolution "respecting the authority of the rendered judgment" and denounced the "odious campaign [to] trouble the public conscience."[1]

At the outset of the revisionist campaign, Millerand had dissociated Socialists from what he considered a bourgeois struggle. He no doubt thought that the Socialist involvement would yield few practical results, especially from an electoral point of view. Still, he was preaching neutrality before the Affair had aroused public passions and in so doing was following Socialist tradition and precept. Socialists had rejected both Boulanger and his Opportunist opposition (see Chapter 1). The policy statement issued by the (Second) International Workingmen's Association in 1891 constituted the orthodox Socialist position. An American Jewish group had asked about the Socialist response to anti-Semitism, and the resolution voted by the association's Brussels Congress clearly subordinated "antagonism or struggle of race or nationality [to] the class struggle between proletarians of all races and capitalists of all races." It merely condemned anti-Semitic agitation as "one of the manoeuvres by which the capitalist class and reactionary governments try to make the Socialist movement deviate and to divide the workers."[2]

Millerand's neutral stand drew criticism from both Dreyfusards and anti-Dreyfusards. The latter upbraided him for not attacking the former, and Drumont accused Millerand and the Socialists of showing leniency to Jewish capitalists. Millerand solidly opposed anti-Semitism (his mother was Jewish), but contended that capitalist exploitation was immoral whether practiced by those who attended the synagogue or those who went to church. Dreyfusards understandably found this attitude incompatible with revolutionary ideals of justice. As early as November 9, 1896, an indignant Bernard-Lazare had written Millerand about an article in the latter's newspaper, *La Petite République*. He found its neutrality "insulting" for a newspaper that professed to be revolutionary and wondered whether it was subsidized by anti-Dreyfusards.[3]

Two months later, thirty-three Socialist deputies signed the manifesto calling on party members to "remain aloof" from bourgeois struggles. Although the proletariat was not insensible to justice, the manifesto stated, it refused to let itself be tricked. Those now invoking the cause of human rights and individual dignity had stolen from workers all the guarantees claimed for Dreyfus. The declaration followed the precedent set four years earlier in January 1893, when the Socialist monthly *La Revue Socialiste* had urged Socialists not to take sides in the Panama Affair. In his history of the Dreyfus Affair and with the mellowness that often accompanies perspective, publicist and leading revisionist Joseph Reinach said that he understood the reasons then given by the Socialists and excused their neutrality. They had fought bitterly against capitalist exploiters and were now being asked to join them.

Millerand's refusal to support the revisionist cause increasingly disturbed the Dreyfusards. His stand angered as well the young Socialist destined for literary fame, Charles Péguy, a staunch Dreyfusard and spokesman for sympathetic students at the prestigious *Ecole Normale*. Péguy resented Socialist neutrality, and especially Millerand's, inasmuch as it emanated from the virtual head of the party.

Péguy sent a steady stream of letters of protest to newspapers and to prominent Socialists. Expressing the sentiments of his fellow *Normaliens*, he labeled Millerand's newspaper anti-Dreyfusard and implored its editorial staff to follow the example now being set by Jaurès. The Socialist party, he cried, could play the role of a great arbiter, but it too has its "general staff" and as one of its chiefs, the "great technician," Alexandre Millerand. Péguy accused Millerand of failing both to safeguard socialism from the "new Boulangists" and to combat the General Staff's attack on individual justice. He was "painfully surprised" to hear of what he called Socialist collaboration with the military.[4]

In his memoirs, Millerand described the dilemma on which French socialism then found itself. On the one hand, he asked, was it not the duty of the party, as Jaurès so eloquently began to plead, to participate in the struggle for justice? On the other, how could it desert the long struggle against capitalism only to join forces with the bourgeoisie in defense of a wealthy army officer convicted by his peers? To a colleague, Millerand wrote that he could not understand Jaurès, who, he said, was "gripped by a veritable frenzy and it was useless to try to reason with him." Millerand agreed with the young Socialist theater critic Léon Blum, who, until his own conversion to the Dreyfusard cause, feared that Jaurès would make socialism unpopular by "irritating public opinion."[5]

The great voice opposing neutrality was now that of Jean Jaurès. Defeated in the 1898 legislative election, he threw himself into editorial work on the Socialist newspaper, *La Petite République*. Once convinced of

Dreyfus's innocence, he viewed the affair not as a simple struggle over the guilt of an officer but one between the progressive elements in the Republic and the organized forces of reaction. During the summer of 1898, he wrote a series of articles, "*Les Preuves*" (The Evidence) to demonstrate Dreyfus's innocence. A number of Socialists converted as well, either to defend the Republic or to conform with their antimilitarist and anticlerical views. Those who did not, like Millerand, continued to stand aside.

All was changed by the confession of Colonel Henry. War Minister Cavaignac was forced to compare samples of Dreyfus's handwriting with that of the alleged confession and, after close examination of the letter reportedly sent by the German military attaché, accepted the possibility of forgery. After Henry's confession and suicide and General Boisdeffre's resignation, the Affair seemed at an end. The entire republican press accepted the need for revision. Most Socialists, including Millerand, now abandoned their neutrality. "On that day," he recalled, "I became an all-out revisionist, with no reservations." Joseph Reinach spoke of the confession as creating "thousands of instantaneous conversions." On that day, he quoted the critic Jules Lemaître: "We all accepted revision."[6]

Jaurès's popularity reached new heights. Incredibly, on the very morning of Henry's confession, he demonstrated in *La Petite République* that the dossier on Dreyfus had to contain a forgery. His renown now equaled that of Zola; he became the leader of the Socialist party, and his name became synonymous with socialism in the mind of the public. As one Socialist deputy suggested, the widespread acclaim for Jaurès may well have paved the way for a Socialist in the government. Another reportedly drank a toast to "the Socialist minister who will inaugurate the next century." Jaurès himself had implicitly predicted executive involvement the previous November. "I believe," he had written at the end of an article in the *Revue Socialiste*, "that the next characteristic of the Socialist movement will consist of more direct and extensive participation on the part of the working class in day-to-day political and social action."[7]

The turmoil created by the Dreyfus Affair and the consequent danger confronting the Republic precipitated a drive to bring together the various Socialist factions. A series of strikes swept through France in the fall of 1898. The government dispatched troops to Paris—by early October, almost an entire army corps. Soldiers occupied railway stations throughout the country. There were rumors of coups by disgruntled army chiefs, rumors easily believed by antimilitarist Socialists. The writer and critic Daniel Halévy has written of the period: "The officers were fidgeting. . . . Who would silence them? . . . The country, leaderless, drifts, with sails slack, like a boat abandoned to the winds." He said that the right hoped to profit from the disorder, judging the time ripe for a coup, and many Frenchmen anticipated a reactionary effort to bring down the regime.[8]

Socialists began to support the regime. Years of parliamentary participation and countless appeals to achieve goals by legal means now bore fruit. They identified with republican institutions and rallied to preserve them. Moderate or Independent Socialists led the way. The Socialist group in the Chamber issued a declaration of protest against the concentration of troops in the Paris area. Revolutionary Marxists pressed the attack for unifying the diverse Socialist factions when they demanded the formation of a permanent central organ, and on October 16 there was created an ad hoc "watch" committee grouping the leading French Socialists and carrying the germs of future unity. The resolutions formulated expressed the intent of the delegates to bring together all revolutionary forces. They would direct their appeal to the proletariat in its entirety, both to protest any infringement of working-class liberties and help defend the Republic. Millerand could not restrain his delight and pride in the latest series of events. In spite of the faults of the bourgeoisie, he wrote, it could rely on workers to safeguard the regime. Although nowhere explicitly suggested, it was probably now that he envisaged an even more effective method of winning Socialist support for the Republic and, at the same time, demonstrating labor's maturity and sense of responsibility: direct governmental participation.

We have seen that on June 3, 1899, France's highest court ordered a new trial and that the next day President Loubet was assaulted by an indignant aristocrat at the Auteuil racetrack. The Progressist government then in office, interrogated on its failure to provide adequate police protection and having lost some of its support, was overthrown, and René Waldeck-Rousseau, a noted corporation lawyer and Progressist senator, was asked to put together a new one. According to Joseph Reinach, who helped advise him, once Waldeck was convinced of the need to form a ministry of "republican defense" and appeal to every political grouping, Millerand, leader of the parliamentary Socialists, appeared as the logical choice to represent "the most advanced opinion." From the standpoint of

Waldeck-Rousseau, an "intelligent conservative," but nonetheless a conservative, Millerand's reformist Socialism was the least disturbing variety.

Why Millerand rather than Jaurès? As Reinach recalled, "Whatever the oratory merits and the political intelligence of Millerand, they would not, however, have sufficed to justify his becoming minister if he had been only a brilliant exception in his party. On the contrary, he was the most representative type, when at that precise moment of Socialist evolution the bulk of the Party had become political and practical, not yet renouncing the impossible, which is the source and motive power of all progress, but attaching itself to the possible and the preferred." Admittedly Jaurès had been one of the leading promoters of that evolution. However, Millerand's role, as observed by Reinach and Waldeck-Rousseau, was even more important in shaping opinion, and he thus seemed the better choice. Governments may use philosophers in formulating the ends to which they aspire, but politicians are usually preferred to carry them out. And as Reinach pointed out, Jaurès, during the Dreyfus Affair, "both in conviction and in timing had preceded the proletariat; Millerand had marched in step with it."[9]

In the interim, rumors flew among Socialists about the possible entry of Millerand (as minister of commerce) into the cabinet being formed, but the prospect aroused no indignation. Independent Socialists welcomed the reports "with pleasure and surprise" and regarded the alleged accession as having "very good effects" and promising "the best results." Militant Socialists also thought in terms of republican defense and were prepared to accept Millerand's entry.

The influence exerted on Jaurès by Lucien Herr, the Socialist librarian of the *Ecole Normale*, had previously persuaded Jaurès that Dreyfus was innocent; he now insisted that the matter of most pressing concern was republican defense. If in order to achieve it this cabinet had been found necessary, they had no choice but to accept the fait accompli. His view in fact corresponded to Jaurès's underlying concept of the vital role projected for socialism in the ideal republic and to his elevation of unity, first Socialist and then republican, as the desired end to which all else was subordinate.

Other party leaders were not so understanding, and revolutionary Marxists were livid. Paul Lafargue, Marx's son-in-law and cofounder of the Marxist faction of the Socialist movement, evoked the concept of the class struggle in condemning Millerand's decision to participate. While acknowl-

edging that Millerand's entry into the government constituted official rec-
ognition of the power of the Socialist movement, which he took pride in,
Lafargue argued that "a socialist in a bourgeois ministry is a socialist lost
to socialism." Because "ministerial participation," as it came to be known,
established a new method of action, he said that Socialists had no choice
but to oppose it. The danger lay in moving socialism from its "true battle-
field" and associating its representatives with the "faults" and "crimes"
committed by bourgeois government. Rather than a Socialist victory, ministerial participation was "a bourgeois trick." As they had done in the Revolution of 1848, the middle class sought to "neutralize" Socialist forces.
Participation, Lagfargue maintained, signified a new tactic, jeopardized the
class struggle, and was incompatible with any effort to establish Socialist
unity on strong theoretical foundations.[10] Their criticism was strengthened
when Millerand, as minister, felt obliged to support such objectionable
government policies as sending troops to the scene of a strike, to defend
government subsidies to religious groups, and to oppose unilateral dis-
armament. These actions ran counter to those of his Socialist colleagues,
which led first to his condemnation by them and ultimately, despite his
efforts to enact measures of social legislation, his expulsion from the party.
Jaurès and the "ministerialist" Socialists who gathered around him maintained that participation was the logical outcome of the policy to win
public power, a policy that had received the support of all Socialists in
the 1893–1898 Chamber. They pointed to the measures of social reform
undertaken by Millerand: France's first social security legislation and
greater rights accorded to trade unions, among others, sought as the natural extension of the reformist tactics previously practiced.

The rest of the Socialist world followed events in France intently. The
particular reaction to them reflected and extended the attitude toward
tactics previously followed. In Great Britain, pragmatic Fabian Socialists,
committed to winning over the existing parties to a more Socialist agenda,
applauded the entry of a Socialist into the government. Similarly, in
Germany, whose Socialist party was the strongest in the world and served
as a model, moderates such as Eduard Bernstein defended Millerand's entry.

On the other hand, radical revolutionaries such as the Polish-born
Rosa Luxemburg and the Russian Vladimir Lenin could not minimize the
importance of what came to be called "the Millerand case" because it went
to the very heart of the Socialist struggle. Socialists can sit in a parliament,

Luxemburg said, but not in a government, for the latter only executes laws and cannot introduce principles. The Socialist in government, if an enemy of the established order, must either be in constant opposition to his colleagues—an untenable position—or he must fulfill his functions, that is, not act as a Socialist, at least not within the limits of government action. The experience, she concluded, appears as one which can only prejudice the principle of the class struggle.[11]

Thus, the Dreyfus Affair, whose resolution required the participation of a Socialist in a government, profoundly affected French—and international—socialism. Indeed, the willingness of most Socialists to support, or at least tolerate, one of their own in a non-Socialist government was a major event in the political history of the past century and a half. Socialists were supposed to defend their class, not their country or their government. Reformist Socialists, beginning with the Dreyfus Affair, came to accept such participation. Revolutionary Socialists, however, continued to reject it. For these revolutionaries, one's attitude toward "ministerialism" came to serve as a test of one's commitment to socialism. Lenin regarded "Millerandism" as the chief threat to Socialist success, and he later denounced Socialists who joined governments during World War I as guilty of deliberate treason. He was to make antiministerialism a test of eligibility for membership in his Communist International, and he deliberately chose the name *Communist* to distinguish revolutionaries like himself from reformists, who kept the name *Socialist* and accepted parliamentary and other democratic strategies. Consequently, the Dreyfus Affair initiated the split between Socialist revolutionaries and Socialists who recognized that with democratic institutions, they might achieve their goals without recourse to revolutionary violence.

Why was this division among Socialists, a division brought on by the Dreyfus Affair, so significant? Because it irreparably weakened the one force, organized labor, that if united might have withstood the onset of twentieth-century fascism in central Europe. But Communists in the late 1920s and early 1930s regarded democratic socialism as a greater threat than fascism. (They interpreted fascism as the last stage of a dying capitalism and saw Nazis, for example, as criminals relied on by capitalists who had forsaken parliamentary means to preserve their assets and had resorted to dictatorship. For many years, Communists would not cooperate in efforts to combat the growing Nazi threat in Germany.) For French socialism, the Millerand case was to guarantee that there would be no government participation by Socialists, aside from temporary inclusion in national unity cabinets formed during the early years of World War I, until the former Dreyfusard Léon Blum formed a ministry in 1936.

Notes

1. Chambre des députés, *Journal Officiel, Débats,* December 4, 1897.

2. Cited in James Joll, *The Second International, 1899–1914* (New York: Harper & Row, 1966), 68.

3. Alexandre Millerand, Unpublished memoirs, Bibliothèque Nationale, Paris.

4. Charles Péguy, "L'Affaire Dreyfus et la crise du parti socialiste," *La Revue Blanche* (1899): 133.

5. Léon Blum, *Souvenirs sur l'affaire* (Paris, 1935), 120.

6. Millerand, memoirs, 36; Joseph Reinach, *Histoire de l'affaire Dreyfus* (Paris, 1901–1908), 4: 222.

7. Jean-Jacques Fiechter, *Le socialisme française: De l'affaire Dreyfus à la Grande Guerre* (Geneva, 1965), 62.

8. Daniel Halévy, "Apologie pour notre passé," *Cahiers de la Quinzaine* (11th series, no. 10): 75, 78.

9. Reinach, *Histoire,* 5: 162.

10. Claude Willard, *Les Guesdistes: le mouvement socialiste en France, 1893–1898* (Paris, 1965), 425–427.

11. Rosa Luxemburg, "Sozial Reform oder Revolution," *Leipziger Volkszeitung,* July 6, 1899. Also published in *Le Mouvement socialiste* (August 1899): 132–133

CHAPTER 5

THE DREYFUS AFFAIR IN HISTORY

The Dreyfus Affair can be viewed as a thrilling detective story, the division of the nation into two hostile camps, and a moral crisis that arose from the conflict between individual justice and the national interest. It was also a decisive episode in the political—as well as in the intellectual and cultural—history of modern France. In their accounts of the Dreyfus Affair, historians have differed over the extent to which one or more of these aspects should be stressed. They differ as well over the conclusions reached but also over the very method of approach. The history of the historical writing about the Dreyfus Affair shows how historians can hold different, and often conflicting, views of the same events.

Those who first wrote about the Dreyfus Affair had participated in it or were old enough to have been profoundly affected by the events that took place, and their histories often reflect the role played or the position taken at the time. Three such writers, two Dreyfusard and one anti-Dreyfusard, were Alexandre Zévaès, Joseph Reinach, and Henri Dutrait-Crozon.

At the time, Zévaès was a Socialist deputy, then an independent social democrat (someone who placed emphasis on social legislation without subscribing to any Socialist theory), who later wrote extensively on the Third Republic. Zévaès became an ardent Dreyfusard (like so many other Socialists, he had initially been neutral), and his account deals harshly with the General Staff, the Church, and other forces seen as reactionary and as creating obstacles in the pursuit of truth and justice. His impassioned account of the Dreyfus Affair, (*L'Affaire Dreyfus*—The Dreyfus Affair, 1931), which did not appear until years later, in 1931, shows how strongly he was affected by it, his reactions were by and large those of the Dreyfusards.

Like many of them, he denounced the General Staff and attributed its moral lapses, readiness to identify Dreyfus as the traitor, and relentless hounding of the unfortunate victim to the anti-Semitism, nationalism, and clericalism of its chiefs. The influence of Drumont's book and newspaper was seen as enormously widespread among army officers, particularly high-ranking ones, as was the nationalist ideal of the writer Maurice Barrès, who appealed to chauvinism and sought the triumph of a military dictatorship. Biographical accounts of Generals Mercier, Boisdeffre, and Gonse, as well as such subordinates as Sandherr, Henry, and du Paty de Clam, show them to be anti-Semites. Zévaès sees the importance of the Jesuit Order as especially strong: Boisdeffre and Gonse, for example, by placing their consciences in the keeping of Father R. P. Dulac of the Company of Jesus, with whom they had "daily conferences." These were the men, Zévaès states, "who put the Dreyfus Affair into operation," for it was their anti-Semitism that led them if not to suspect an artillery officer on probation to the General Staff, then "to stop at once at the name of Dreyfus" when consulting the list of such officers. The response of Sandherr is indicative: "A Jew! I should have known it" (21).

No further questions were asked. Although the author of the *bordereau* had written that he was "going on maneuvres," no one inquired whether Dreyfus had gone on maneuvers. Moreover, the terms used in it to describe the new artillery pieces were inaccurate (for example, using "hydraulic brake" for "hydropneumatic brake" and writing "120" instead of "120 limited"; anyone with technical training would have used the correct designation. But these anti-Semitic officers "were too proud, too happy with their discovery to pause at such trifles." And far from taking alarm at the excitement of the press, whose indictment of Dreyfus was, to say the least, premature, War Minister Mercier "sought to reinforce the violence at the same time that he was instructing members of the court-martial how to vote" (32).

Joseph Reinach's penetrating analysis of Mercier (*Histoire de l'Affaire Dreyfus*—History of the Dreyfus Affair, 7 vols., 1901–1911) has been used by the authors of later published accounts. That the general's star was fading, that his errors generated misgivings and disappointment, that he was viewed by both anticlericals and anti-Semites as a demagogue interested only in pursuing a political career, and that he saw a vigorous pursuit of Dreyfus as the vehicle by which he could rehabilitate himself have all been accepted as legitimate motivations for his behavior. The *bordereau* had been discovered. If the traitor remained undetected, Mercier's career, already jeopardized, would come to an end. He must be found, and when Dreyfus was named, Mercier worked relentlessly to have him condemned and deported.

Reinach claimed that a French agent retrieved the *bordereau* from the concierge's desk before it ever reached Schwartzkoppen; that on receiving it, Henry recognized the handwriting as that of Esterhazy, a close friend for twenty years; and that either because Henry was Esterhazy's accomplice in treason or simply his friend, Henry tore it up, pasted it back together, and maintained that it came from the "usual track"—Madame Bastian's gatherings from the embassy wastebasket. (Henry could not simply destroy it because the agent who delivered it would speak to his superiors about his find.) Schwartzkoppen insisted that he had never received the *bordereau*. But he would not have wanted to admit his incompetence in throwing documents away or be forced to acknowledge his involvement in espionage without having informed the German ambassador. He doubtless feared the disclosure of a flirtatious and probably homosexual relationship that existed between him and his Italian counterpart, Panizzardi (as revealed in documentation that found its way to French Intelligence). Reinach's representation of Henry as Esterhazy's accomplice was a staple Dreyfusard belief but has been rejected by subsequent historians. Still, Reinach's factual narrative, in contrast to some of his interpretations and speculations, has endured.

The anti-Dreyfusard analysis, certainly the one wholly accepted by those opposed to revision, is the 700-page précis of the Affair published under the name Henri Dutrait-Crozon in 1909 and subsequently republished. Dutrait-Crozon was the pseudonym used by two French colonels, Georges Louis Larpent and Frédéric Delebecque. The second edition of their book has become the definitive one and presents the most forceful summation of the anti-Dreyfusard case (*Précis de l'Affaire Dreyfus*—A Summary of the Dreyfus Affair, 1924). The authors agreed on the national interest as the supreme consideration and so assumed that any diminution of that interest, particularly on behalf of a Jewish officer convicted of treason, necessarily originated in the work of a powerful and traitorous organization, one with resources great enough to bribe the corrupt Esterhazy to confess to a crime he did not commit.

The colonels point to the "powerful espionage" undertaken by the German and Italian military attachés and the steps taken to combat it by French Intelligence. The arrival of the *bordereau* was only the latest indication of it, and the investigating officers were on solid ground in assuming the traitor was an artillery officer serving as a trainee on the General Staff. They recalled that Dreyfus had received a poor evaluation, compared his handwriting with that of the *bordereau*, and were "stupefied" at the resemblance. But only after further comparisons carefully made with other documents did they inform the deputy chief of staff, General Gonse. The procedures leading to Dreyfus's arrest and indictment were therefore proper and legitimate. The secret dossier sent to the judges, consisting of these documents and of commentaries on them, "hardly influenced the judges; their decision to convict was obtained from the arguments presented" (36–38).

The authors argue that after the condemnation of Dreyfus, a Jewish conspiracy, grouping Mathieu Dreyfus, Picquart, and Esterhazy, was launched to reopen the case. Picquart was "instructed to get his superiors to substitute Esterhazy for Dreyfus." To have Esterhazy's handwriting appear identical to that of the *bordereau*, he worked assiduously to imitate it and to have himself assigned to the Ministry of War in order to claim previous contact with officers of the ministry and access to the documents listed in the *bordereau*. Simultaneously Mathieu began his press campaign "to intimidate the Minister of War and the Chief of Staff." Esterhazy was in no real danger, for in view of the widespread belief in Dreyfus's guilt, he could count on acquittal by a court-martial. Then secure (he could not be tried again for the same crime), he would be able "to continue openly his activities in favor of Dreyfus, even to declare that he had written the *bordereau*" (49–50, 102).

This thesis—that Esterhazy was the straw-man of the Jews—was for anti-Dreyfusards "the key to the Dreyfus Affair." The difficulty, of course, is that there is no credible evidence to support the idea that a well-placed Jewish conspiracy was responsible for Mathieu's propaganda campaign, Picquart's revelation, and Esterhazy's conviction. The authors assume that because the Dreyfusard campaign appeared so well organized, because extensive financial backing was required, because the president of a Committee of Defense against anti-Semitism was born of a Prussian father, because bankrupt newspapers revived after taking a Dreyfusard stand, because Esterhazy died wealthy, a powerful Jewish syndicate was behind it all, an argument long believed by those unable to accept the fact that Dreyfus had been wrongly accused and that different people rose to his defense.

Belief in conspiracy was not limited to anti-Dreyfusard writers. Some historians, like most of the revisionists, have insisted on the presence of a reactionary clerico-military plot to overthrow the existing Republic. One such writer is Jacques Kayser (*The Dreyfus Affair*, 1931), and like Zévaès (who published at about the same time), he also places stress on anti-Semitism as making intelligible the early assumption of guilt on the part of Dreyfus's superiors. Kayser, a newspaperman, was actively involved in politics. He was former editor of the newspaper *La République*, wrote for the prestigious daily *Le Monde*, and served as secretary-general of the Radical-Socialist party. He published histories of radicalism and the provincial press during the Third Republic and a life of Lafayette.

By placing the event in its larger political context, Kayser shows how insecure the Third Republic was, how many of the French saw it as a mere transitional arrangement when it was established, and how hostile many remained to it. He noted how its opponents made use of the numerous affairs and scandals, ranging from the efforts of the son-in-law of an early president to traffic in Legion of Honor decorations to the bribes taken by deputies from the company trying to build a canal in Panama. Immorality, instability, corruption, and decadence seemed to mark the Republic, whose defenders appeared weak, irresolute, and incapable. "A reactionary nationalist movement," Kayser states, "was taking shape, directed at once outwards against the foreigner, and especially against Germany, inwards against the Jew, represented as a profiteer and the agent of the foreigner, and the socialist, as the creation of disorder." Order could be maintained only by the Army; morality, only by the Church; and the generals and the bishops colluded to bring down the Republic and destroy the liberals and the Jews who supported it. And underlying their common exertions were the "the unwearying efforts of the Jesuits, those implacable and irreconcilable enemies of modern and republican ideas." The case of treason provided the enemies of the Republic with their opportunity: they could launch a great counter-offensive and regain their grip on the country. The political battle of the reactionaries and the clericals was underway.

Even so, in the 1930s, conservative historians, particularly those holding out chances for a monarchist restoration and revival of the

Church's authority, upheld the sincerity of the General Staff and found Dreyfus guilty, thus invalidating any confession made by Esterhazy and regretting the growth of "radicalism" in the wake of the Affair. Such is the interpretation made by Jacques Bainville. He wrote extensively on French history in a characteristically concise and terse style. Intensely conservative, he contributed numerous articles to the monarchist and nationalist *Action Française*. Because of his histories, particularly the works on Napoleon, he was elected to the Académie Française in 1935, the year before his death. In his history of the Third Republic (*La Troisième République*—The Third Republic, 1935), he presented a more balanced conservative analysis of the Dreyfus Affair than did Dutrait-Crozon, although his conclusions do not significantly differ.

Like Dutrait-Crozon, he acknowledged the German efforts to discover French military capabilities. The creation of an "espionage agency" at the German embassy is not left in doubt, nor is the authenticity of the *bordereau*. Clearly, yet another traitor was at large. Only by a process of elimination was Dreyfus identified as the culprit. The guilty verdict of the judges was legitimately arrived at and accepted by the government. The wrong, in view of the harm inflicted on the nation, lay in its repeal. It would have been better to have watched Dreyfus until he was caught in the act, but it was easier and less honest to get rid of him at once. The General Staff was guilty of having scruples; it could have sent him to a colony "from which one does not return" (194–197).

For Bainville, Mathieu Dreyfus secured help from "sensitive or generous souls" troubled by a possible injustice and from those who made "reparation of the injustice a question of conscience and honor for the French." While awaiting new evidence to break the 1894 verdict, Dreyfus's defenders claimed that an innocent man had been unjustly and illegally condemned, although even Jaurès admitted the necessity of secret documents in a treason trial. Bainville distinguished the courage of the first Dreyfusards from the opportunism of the "eleventh hour workers" (198-199).

Esterhazy was acquitted because his accusers lacked proof of his guilt, and once found innocent he could admit to having written the *bordereau*. (He knew he could not again be prosecuted for a crime of which he was acquitted.) Anti-Dreyfusards had no difficulty in recognizing that a man capable of treason could "assume the guilt in order to render service to another," and so Bainville subscribed to the Dutrait-Crozon thesis. Henry's confession and suicide were seen as irrelevant to the 1894 trial inasmuch as his forgeries were committed after that judgment. If it persuaded many of Dreyfus's innocence, its juridical value was null.

Catholic organizations were asked for help, and if they were not forthcoming with help, threatened that anticlericals and Socialists would be turned to, making the Republic back away from the *ralliement* and the reconciliation it promised. The Church understandably refused to join in an attack against the army, and so Socialists and "all who had an interest in disorder and in taking revenge" entered the fray.

When Esterhazy confessed, Bainville wrote, he did so "on orders," and his refusal to testify at Rennes was bizarrely agreed to by both parties. Not even a deposition was requested from him, and Bainville could not understand why it was necessary to reopen the case if Dreyfus's innocence was revealed by Esterhazy's guilt. He found the judges' second guilty verdict understandable in view of the prosecution's witnesses, who demonstrated that "as in 1894 the traitor could only be in the artillery, and was an officer and trainee on the General Staff." He described their concession of "extenuating circumstances" as evidence of their "wish to appease" and explained Jaurès's "tenacity" in seeking rehabilitation for Dreyfus as driven by the desire "to maintain the revolutionary agitation which had proven so profitable for the progressive (i.e., Socialist and Radical) parties." Even the publication of Schwartzkoppen's memoirs could not persuade Bainville of Dreyfus's total innocence (216–219).

With few exceptions, historians writing after World War II, perhaps influenced by the growing acceptance of social science methodologies, saw the issue less as angels confronting devils, as did the partisans, and preferred to focus on analyzing the structures, or the mechanisms, involved. Accordingly, such writers as the Englishman Guy Chapman and the Frenchman Marcel Thomas chose to deemphasize the personal guilt or innocence of the leading protagonists and to discuss and evaluate the Intelligence Service, the General Staff, the Church, and Parliament as institutions, and the activities of the protagonists chiefly within these frameworks or structures.

The distinguished historian and political scientist François Goguel, in his important handbook for the study of the Third Republic (*La Politique des Partis sous la IIIe République*—Party Politics under the Third Republic, 1946), explains the attitude of Picquart's superiors, who dismissed the evidence of Esterhazy's guilt contained in the *petit-bleu*. They did so in terms of "an oversimplified conception of discipline" and the conviction that "an officer discredits himself in acknowledging a mistake." Despite the proofs that led Scheurer-Kestner to demand that the case be reopened, the Méline government refused. It did so not only because it believed Dreyfus guilty but because it feared that revision would "unleash agitation which might prove fatal to it, in arousing the opposition of those Catholics who had supported Drumont's anti-Semitic campaign" (pp. 88–89).

Goguel also supported what has come to be known as the "two culprit" or "third man" theory belatedly asserted by Esterhazy. Articulated by anti-Dreyfusards, it would be given new life by the posthumous journal of the diplomat Maurice Paléologue, whose *Journal de l'Affaire Dreyfus* (Journal of the Dreyfus Affair, 1955) suggests that the real author of the *bordereau* would have been a high-ranking secret agent of the French intelligence service, or Mercier's *chef de cabinet* (cabinet director), General Rau, or, as stated in yet another attempt to identify the third man (Henri Giscard d'Estaing, *De Dreyfus à Esterhazy*—From Dreyfus to Esterhazy, 1960), Mercier himself. According to this theory, Esterhazy, not Dreyfus, was selling secrets to the Germans. "However," Goguel argued, "it is difficult to believe that he was guilty of all the acts of which Dreyfus was accused" (98). This proposition of the anti-Dreyfusards was never wholly refuted. The "departure for maneouvres" referred to in the *bordereau* "corresponds to no known episode in Esterhazy's life. Nor was he in a position to obtain the documents listed." Hence, Goguel saw a need to suppose the existence of two culprits, and he agrees with Bainville that the publication of Schwartzkoppen's memoirs failed to resolve the issue. The latter's notebooks point to Dreyfus's innocence but fail to name the guilty party.

Someone besides Esterhazy, then, delivered documents to the German embassy. Dreyfus's conviction protected the other traitor, who therefore tried to "reinforce" the dossier compiled against the Jewish officer and so prevent having the case reopened. Goguel admits all this is only a hypothesis, but doubts that certainty, unless new evidence emerged, could ever be reached. In the interim, the guilt of both Esterhazy and a third party was the explanation that "best agrees with the established facts while, at the same time, clears up those which remain obscure" (pp. 99–100).

Guy Chapman, a former professor at the University of Leeds and author of two books on the Dreyfus Affair, also plays down the importance attached to individual motives or, more precisely, situates them in a larger structural context. In *The Dreyfus Case* (1955), he rejects unconditionally the notion of a clerico-military conspiracy and deflates enormously the influence of anti-Semitism, which "no doubt existed, but it cannot be shown to have played a dominant part in the arrest and trial of Dreyfus." For Chapman, the Dreyfus Affair was the result of a legitimate error committed by the General Staff, and the case is thus relegated to causes wholly accidental (p. 9).

In his analysis of the army, Chapman rejects republican—and Dreyfusard—claims that those who accused Dreyfus of treason opposed the republican regime itself. When drawn into civil crises—in 1830, 1848, 1851, and 1871—officers had always obeyed the orders of their highest authority, the minister of war. It was republicans who in the late 1870s, having purged non-republican elements in the civil service, "had given the vacant places to their friends and parasites." In the early 1880s, they did the same with the judiciary. Only on the army they "had not laid their sacrilegious hands." But the royalists who made it something of a preserve, were not necessarily practicing Catholics (even if they were believers), and the officer class was at best "neutral towards the regime." Clericalism played a minimal part in promotions, despite talk by "the politicians and press of the Left" of a clerico-military plot. In the May 1877 crisis, the Boulanger episode, and Déroulède's attempted coup of February 1899, the army played little or no part.

Similarly, Chapman sees little evidence to back the claim of anticlerical writers that, save for the Assumptionist Order, the Church was allied with the army in a conspiracy against the Republic. A few exceptions do not make the rule, he argues, and the Jesuits were singled out because of their "romantic reputation for conspiracy." Reinach's charges of Jesuit-based anti-Semitism are based on "the flimsiest of evidence"—a single "foolish" anti-Semitic article—and he ignored an equally violent polemic against the Church printed previously in a Jewish newspaper that prompted the article (pp. 18, 200–201).

Dreyfus himself is portrayed as remarkably unsympathetic: wealthy, vain, and narrow. That he was disliked and not that he was Jewish accounted for the hostile testimony of his fellow officers. As stated, anti-Semitism "cannot be shown to have played a dominant part in the arrest and trial of Dreyfus." Chapman denies that the Affair was a morality play. The more the evidence is examined," he asserts, "the less heroic and the less odious do the leading actors become. Far from a battle between good and evil, the case, when "cool[ly] examin[ed], shows that in its origins it arose partly from genuine error or deception, partly from mistaken loyalty." Henry's forgeries issued from his loyalty to the military, and his suicide allowed the politicians to reveal how opportunistic they were. Chapman found their subsequent display of virtue "as revolting as their unscrupulous attacks on the Church and the Army and their creation of the fantasy of a clerico-military plot." And he concludes that because "nine tenths" of the histories of the Dreyfus Affair are pro-Dreyfus, the Dreyfusard view, with its crude blacks and whites, has passed into history. (The anti-Dreyfusard versions, Chapman admits, are equally distorted, but because their side lost, they are ineffective.) The Affair was not one of "virtue" versus "villainy" but of "fallible human beings" pulled by "beliefs," "loyalties," "prejudices," "ambition," and "ignorance."

Some readers regretted what they considered as a lack of indignation on Chapman's part and the unnecessarily dry and analytic approach taken to this classic case of a miscarriage of justice. Seventeen years later Chapman republished his findings (*The Dreyfus Trials*, 1972), a volume in a Historical Trials series, which critics found "more compelling" than its predecessor. Both sides in the Affair are still dealt with harshly, and the earlier distinction made between Dreyfusist (defined as those who at the outset suspected a judicial error and sought to reopen the case) and Dreyfusard (a term coined by opponents of revision who opportunistically used the Affair for political or personal advantage) remain as sharp as ever. Moreover, the author restates his conclusions that the Affair did not assume national prominence until 1899, that it was not driven by anti-Semitism, and that the Republic was not threatened by the military.

The history of the Dreyfus Affair that places most emphasis on structural and psychological analyses is that of Marcel Thomas (*L'Affaire sans Dreyfus*—The Affair without Dreyfus, 1961). Thomas was the conservator of the Bibliothèque Nationale, France's national library, and he wrote with authority on subjects ranging from the trial of Mary Stuart to the exploits of Roland. In his account of the Dreyfus Affair, he was able to make use of material long believed to have been destroyed in two world wars, specifically the documents accumulated by General Gonse (which demonstrated without doubt his and du Paty's complicity) as well as the secret dossier sent to the 1894 court-martial. Thomas minimizes the private motives of the leading characters and passes over the personal role of

Captain Dreyfus, whom he describes as until 1899 "the least informed man in the world" (13).

Much of what happened, Thomas insists, may be explained by "the very special mentality ultimately acquired by those who belong, in no matter what capacity, to the secret services"—here, the Statistical Section. Their esprit de corps implanted within them a distrust of, and an attitude of condescension toward, other departments and agencies, particularly those run by civilians, an attitude not unusual on the part of higher-ranking police officials. Its chief, who alone knew all its personnel and sources of information and believed himself personally bound to his sources and obliged not to reveal them, felt no need to account to anyone. In addition, the "chronic disorder" of the Intelligence Service, the "deplorable negligence," "the haste, the confusion which marked the first inquiries" contributed significantly to "muddle things" and compound mistakes (71–72).

Anti-Semitism, argues Thomas, did not explain why Dreyfus was suspected but did explain why the idea of his guilt was more easily accepted. The subconscious prejudice and the "anti-Semitic reflex" helped tilt "the heavy ministerial machine in the direction of the error." Mercier's decision to prosecute was taken in good faith, but once it was set in motion, he could not reverse the process without damaging his career. On the other hand, the minister of foreign affairs, Gabriel Hanotaux, could not permit the disclosure of information stolen from a foreign embassy. Such disclosure would justifiably generate German protests, and France's first diplomat voiced opposition even to continuing the investigation. Mercier persuaded Prime Minister Dupuy to allow the proceedings to continue, but (on Hanotaux's insistence) the prime minister secured a promise that they would be abandoned if other proof beside the *bordereau* was not found—hence, the origin of the secret dossier and the forged and irrelevant documents. "Once released, the wheels of the diabolical mechanism . . . began to turn, and one sees why the General Staff refused to divulge its methods of work" (pp. 158–159).

Thomas acknowledges that generals who accepted the "martyrdom of an innocent man" in order to avoid a scandal could be charged with "atrocious cowardice." Yet he reminds us that "these generals did not and could not believe in Dreyfus's innocence, and there will always be those who prefer injustice to disorder." Here, however, their decision could only create disorder and perpetuate injustice (278).

In an appendix, Thomas discusses—and refutes—as legend the "third man" thesis. He rejects as well Reinach's speculation about the arrival of the *bordereau*. The latter arrived by "the usual route," that is, by way of Madame Bastian. But the General Staff long concealed her role in order to keep her activities as secret as possible. No French agent retrieved it before Schwartzkoppen saw it. Henry, if Esterhazy's accomplice, could have destroyed the *bordereau* without fear of being blackmailed by the agent who supposedly retrieved it (an explanation Reinach had to invent to explain why it was not destroyed, given his conviction that Henry was an accomplice to Esterhazy's treason). For Thomas, Henry did not destroy it because he was not an accomplice, and no less a well-placed person than Picquart refused to believe that he was. Schwartzkoppen's denial of ever having seen the *bordereau* is entirely understandable: he would scarcely admit to having failed to take the most basic precautions, of having had his letters stolen for so long by an illiterate maid.

Another historian of this generation, one who similarly tried to analyze the structures, or rather, movements and institutions of French society, is Douglas Johnson (*France and the Dreyfus Affair*, 1966). The author of a study of Guizot (the Orléanist minister who urged the discontent to "get rich" so they too could vote), Johnson asks why a judicial injustice developed into an "affair" that embroiled the nation. His reply—that "it corresponded to something peculiar within France" rather than "the alignment of the forces of right fighting against the forces of wrong"—requires a study of the cultural and intellectual climate (and the forces that helped to shape it): nationalism; militarism, and especially those involved in counterespionage; the intellectuals; the press; and anti-Semitism (7). All these things, Johnson believes, can be attributed to widespread feelings of insecurity. The "spy mania" that swept the intelligence service was understandable given France's determination to prepare for possible war. But the plethora of agents and would-be agents contained "unreliable elements" and generated uncertainty. The efforts of the Statistical Section to collect "every scrap of paper," the officers who took classified documents home to work on them, and the departmental and personal rivalries all led to inefficiency and mistakes. Esterhazy's *bordereau* was intended to call attention to its author and justify German payments to him. It referred only to "general, journalistic-type articles," and French intelligence officers erroneously believed it promised to deliver "precise and confidential documents." Then they mistakenly concluded that only an important staff officer could have written it, and from such mistakes the case mushroomed into the Affair.

Not the consequence of a conspiracy, the Dreyfus Affair was rather "a series of logical mistakes, made by a number of people who were both over-credulous and over-suspicious and taking place in a community where such mistakes could not easily be recognized or rectified" (207).

Similarities abound between Dreyfusards and anti-Dreyfusards. If the latter attacked Dreyfus as a Jew, the former attacked Esterhazy as a foreigner; if the latter denounced the Jewish "syndicate," the former inveighed against the clerico-military syndicate organized by the Jesuits; and if Drumont condemned the judges for turning pro-Dreyfusard to advance their careers, Clemenceau condemned the generals for the same reason. The difference between anti-Dreyfusards and Dreyfusards was real, Johnson states, but it was "not one of personality, of scruples, or of methods." An examination of the relevant institutions suggests that it was usually a minority who strongly opposed—or defended—Dreyfus. The Assumptionists, Jesuits, and parish priests who denounced Dreyfus differed from the majority of Catholics, who, like the hierarchy, seemed indifferent. Many Socialists found Jaurès too enthusiastic and continued to dismiss the Affair as a bourgeois quarrel (211–212).

Majorities were involved only when responsive chords were struck. Anti-Semitism had a long tradition in France and was related to social and national insecurity, particularly that of the "smaller bourgeoisie." In an explanation many historians accept for the rise of fascism, this group felt isolated because of a stagnant economy and their precarious position between a rising labor force and big business. They feared that foreign competition would devastate small industry, small agriculture, and small commerce. Out of this "almost permanent insecurity" emerged a reinvigorated anti-Semitism—a collection of resentments, fears, and xenophobia that the Dreyfus case was able to crystallize because "it dramatically presented the Jew in two of his traditional roles, that of conspirator and that of traitor" (213–214).

Related to anti-Semitism as a majority movement and emerging from an equally old tradition, and also seen as an expression of national insecurity, were nationalism and militarism, both based on a realization of how divided the country was and how necessary it was to achieve unity. Symbolizing this unity was the French army. The intellectual crisis of the 1890s was reflected in the attack on positivism and rationalism as embodied in religious revivalism, irrationalism, and nationalism. Johnson describes this new intellectual climate as especially relevant to the French bourgeoisie and responsible for the moral crisis through which it was passing.

Finally, and in contrast to the theories of Goguel, Johnson finds that there is simply insufficient evidence to support notions of the third man— the theory that because Dreyfus was not guilty and because Esterhazy could not have been guilty of all the acts of treason of which he was accused, there had to be a third man, still undiscovered, who was also guilty and helped persuade the General Staff that Dreyfus was the traitor and that the case should not be reopened. If there were any real evidence, Mercier's chief of staff, General Rau, could not have continued to serve in impor- tant political and military capacities. Nor could Mercier himself have built a private intelligence operation—and ordered Esterhazy to write the *bor- dereau* to send false information to the Germans—without Sandherr and the Statistical Section (who were doing the same thing) knowing about it. These theories, then, not only lack supporting evidence; they are "in- herently improbable" (201–205).

The social-psychological dimensions of the Dreyfus Affair were ex- plored in the 1955 best-seller by Nicholas Halasz (*Captain Dreyfus: The Story of a Mass Hysteria*) that describes the disorder and passion in the struggle between Dreyfusards and anti-Dreyfusards. As suggested in the subtitle, the writer, who served as foreign correspondent for European and American newspapers, stressed the hysterical fervor that swept over the nation and transformed and disrupted all aspects of daily life (a scope con- tradicted by Chapman, who, we have seen, limits the discord, at least until 1899, to Paris).

Halasz, however, sees the Affair as no less than a "morality play that was to achieve a grandeur unparalleled in the history of the modern state" (5), one that pitted those defending justice for an individual against those who proclaimed priority for what they perceived as the national interest. Numerous examples of how private lives and concerns gave way to ideo- logical commitment are provided. Few nuances are offered: it was "only a handful" (a stubborn clique in the view of the vast majority opposing re- vision) who initially kept faith in democracy. They were confronted by "the Army," "the aristocracy," and "the parish priests of five thousand churches throughout France [who] echoed the battle cry" and reinforced "the tidal wave of anti-Semitism that swept over the country." Still, in describing the "unrest" that almost brought to a "standstill" the pursuits of public and private life in France, substituting for them "meetings, demonstrations, brawls, debates, the organizing of coups d'états and of forces to forestall them, [and the breakup] of families and friendships forever," Halasz's attempts to portray the society as gripped in moral fervor makes for dramatic reading and highlights an added dimension (124–125, 136).

Most recently, the Dreyfus Affair continues to attract attention from distinguished—and not so distinguished—writers. Because almost all that can be said on the sequence of events has been said, particularly by Marcel Thomas, little new information has been forthcoming. The subject matter discusses the significance of the Affair and explores the contexts in which it took place: the press, the army, the Church, anti-Semitism, the political and social settings, and biographies of Dreyfus and his family and Bernard-Lazare. (See the Annotated Bibliography for a sampling of those works not discussed here.) The role of anti-Semitism in particular has undergone a revival in recent years. There seems little doubt that the vast number of publications and films, both scholarly and popular, on the Holocaust has prompted historians to reevaluate the hostility shown to Jews at the time of the Dreyfus Affair.

Michael Burns's well-written *Dreyfus: Family Affair* (1991) traces the Dreyfus family tree, beginning with his ancestors in the eighteenth century, followed by a biography of Alfred, a subject neglected by historians of the Affair inasmuch as the victim for so long was totally isolated from events, and ending with a family history down to 1945. The story is filled out with interesting, if not always entirely relevant, asides: a description of the Paris Exposition of 1900 and a discussion of electricity magnate Ernest Mercier's French Renewal Movement that sought to promote the modernization of the economy. (Alfred's niece married Mercier after her first husband, Joseph Reinach's son, was killed early in World War I.) Nelly Wilson's *Bernard-Lazare: Anti-Semitism and the Problem of Jewish Identity in Late Nineteenth Century France* (1978), the best biography in English, attempts to rescue its subject from anonymity and make his role a central one in the Dreyfusard movement. She traces his intellectual development from symbolist poet to journalist and literary anarchist. If Wilson's contention that Dreyfus owed his freedom to Bernard-Lazare's convictions and commitment is overstated, Lazare's important role in the Affair, particularly that of helping to create an "international moral syndicate" working for Dreyfus, is well defended. David Lewis, *Prisoners of Honor* (1973), is a popularly written account, which despite the claim to have used a wide variety of sources, including interviews with descendants, does not add much in the way of new information or interpretation. As suggested in the title, both accused and accusers believed they were defending honor, in the one case, that of the prisoner himself and his family; in the other, that of the nation.

"Third man" theses have proliferated in the recent literature. Co-incidentally, after Goguel published his speculations on the subject, Maurice Paléologue, at the time in charge of intelligence matters at the Ministry of Foreign Affairs and ordered to follow the Dreyfus case for his superiors' edification, posthumously published his memoirs in 1955 (*Journal de l'Affaire Dreyfus* [Journal of the Dreyfus Affair]). He conceived of three culprits: Esterhazy; Maurice Weil, an ambitious and brilliant but corrupt (Jewish) officer who befriended him; and an unnamed "extremely high-ranking officer." There is no evidence, however, that Weil, however unscrupulous and short of funds, committed treason (supposedly with Saussier's protection or even complicity), yet the scenario proved attractive to anti-Dreyfusards because it replaced a Jew with a Jew.[1]

Other historians exonerate the General Staff. For Michel de Lombarès (*L'Affaire Dreyfus: La Clef du Mystère* [The Dreyfus Affair: The Key to the Mystery], 1972), the *bordereau* was fabricated by German counter-espionage from notes that Esterhazy, a French spy feeding false information to the Germans, gave to Schwartzkoppen. The Germans wanted to ensure that Esterhazy was not a double agent: if French intelligence reacted when getting the *bordereau*, that would show that Esterhazy was truly working for the Germans. Yet another writer, Henri Giscard d'Estaing (*D'Esterhazy à Dreyfus* [From Esterhazy to Dreyfus], 1950) also sees Esterhazy as a double agent sent to give the Germans false or useless information. Once Dreyfus was suspected, however, Mercier and the French generals could not reveal their secret network and so had to let an innocent man suffer.

Perhaps the most acclaimed of the latest studies of the Dreyfus Affair is that of Jean-Denis Bredin (*The Affair: The Case of Alfred Dreyfus*, 1986). Bredin has a background in history and law, which helps account for his mastery of the legal processes. Like Johnson, he places the Affair in the larger context of French history, including that of a rising tide of anti-Semitism. Indeed, the book argues that because the terrain was favorable, the Dreyfus Affair was "well rooted" in its time.

The "time" is described in well-placed chapters, or sections of chapters, at appropriate locations in the narrative: on the army (a preserve for royalist high-ranking officers), on anti-Semitism (which burgeoned after 1880), on Boulangism (which like the Dreyfus Affair emerged in times of significant social change), on a collective mentality (that saw the 1871 defeat as a consequence of betrayals and justified espionage and counter-espionage activities), and on the press (which ultimately strengthened the Republic and democracy—without Clemenceau's *L'Aurore*, Dreyfus would have remained in prison, although without Drumont's *Libre Parole*, he might not have been sent there). These analyses are inserted into the narrative, as are discussions of how historians have interpreted the events described (as, for example, the conflicting theses concerning the arrival of the *bordereau*).

Bredin rejects the many legends about these events as having been invented in their entirety or fabricated on the basis of doctored clues—among them, that Dreyfus confessed after the degradation ceremony, that the *bordereau* was annotated by the kaiser, that there was a Jewish syndicate conspiring to overturn the guilty verdict, and that Henry did not really commit suicide but was assassinated by a masked intruder. These legends were supported by lies, exaggerations, or self-serving liberties (such as Schwartzkoppen understandably denying he threw important documents into a wastebasket). Like Thomas, Bredin rejects the thesis of three guilty parties advanced by Paléologue and others.

His bibliography is remarkably thorough, going beyond the traditional breakdown of primary and secondary sources. Secondary works are listed under such categories as "Intellectuals," "Army," "Literature and the Dreyfus Affair," "The Role of the Press," and "Anti-Semitism." Picquart is seen as a hero who saw the truth "and never wavered from it." The Affair, Bredin insists, truly began when the newspaper *L'Eclair*, in an anti-Dreyfusard article triggered by the rumor of Dreyfus's escape, asserted that the case against Dreyfus was airtight, and in so doing revealed that a secret dossier had been sent to the judges in the 1894 court-martial but never shown to the defense. Lucie Dreyfus's appeal based on the disclosure of this irregularity was widely published, making more people aware of how the process was tampered with.

Like the writing of much other history, then, that about the Dreyfus Affair has been subject to revision. The early accounts, particularly those of the players in the drama, while providing useful information, tended to portray events in stark and glaring terms and did not hesitate to assign blame, whether to Dreyfus or to his accusers. Although some later historians still wrote in similar ways, most have preferred to place emphasis on the contexts in which these events unfolded. Most condemn the people who persecuted an innocent man, but their condemnation aims at fallible and deluded human beings, however cowardly their behavior.

Note

1. Henri Guillemin, *L'Enigme Esterhazy* (Paris,1962), names General Félix Saussier, the military governor of Paris and the de facto commander-in-chief of the French armed forces, as the "third man," whose protection extended from Weil to Esterhazy. Guillemin admits this is only a hypothesis, as is his speculation that it was Sandherr, as Esterhazy maintained, who dictated the *bordereau* to him in hopes that Saussier would recognize the script of his protégé and be more careful. If so, the gambit failed because other officers noted the similarity with Dreyfus's handwriting.

CHAPTER 6

CONCLUSION

How influential was the Dreyfus Affair in French history? The coalition of left-wing Progressists, Radicals, and Socialists who gathered in support of Waldeck-Rousseau's government of national defense hardened into a politically dominant movement directed by a powerful steering committee, the *Délégation des Gauches*, that was to govern France until World War I. Whether this Dreyfusard success and the Dreyfus Affair that brought it about marked a turning point in the history of France's Third Republic or whether it simply "speeded up a movement in French politics which had been gathering force since the beginning of the last decade of the nineteenth century," has been open to controversy.[1] That the Affair enabled the left to come to power and push through legislation reflecting its priorities, particularly those of anticlericalism and antimilitarism, and at least the promise of enough social legislation to bring significant elements of Socialists and labor to the support of the Republic, cannot be doubted.

Waldeck-Rousseau, the prime minister who pardoned Dreyfus, however, saw himself as "a moderate republican but not moderately republican." A man of order, he distanced himself from the far left as much as from the far right. He intended to control the most outspoken anti-Republican religious orders and not to bring about separation of church and state. It may well be that he regarded the lack of discipline within the army, and the insubordination revealed by some of its chiefs, as the most pressing danger. Hence, his first cabinet decision was to appoint as war minister the prestigious General Galliffet precisely because this general possessed the authority to impose discipline. The leader of the parliamentary Socialists, Millerand, would balance Galliffet and ensure at least the neutrality, if not the support, of the far left. Seen from this perspective, it was

Waldeck's wish to shelter the army from the vengeance of the newly em-
powered Dreyfusards that explained his amnesty bill, which protected the
most compromised generals from indictment. To compensate, and to protect the army further, he would have to make concessions to the majority
by seeking an alternate target. Clericalism at once came to mind because
the male religious congregations had favored the anti-Republican right and
so was an enemy waiting to be attacked. Any blows aimed at it would be
applauded by all republicans, and anticlericalism would thus hold together
his heterogeneous coalition of "republican defense."

Admittedly, the prime minister sought to neutralize the Church's
political power. The periodic attacks against the Republic in 1877, 1889,
and 1899 had invariably contained factions of the Church and had won
the approval of high-ranking officers in the army. Galliffet's successor,
General André, was seeking to republicanize the army; it was now to be
the turn of the most belligerent congregations. But it was the need to preserve the army as a force capable of defending France that accounted for
the government's efforts to limit the church's power. There may also be
some truth in the interpretation of the spate of anticlerical legislation in
the first few years of the new century as another attempt on the part of
business interests to divert systematically to the religious orders animosities
directed against themselves. In any case, there seems little doubt that
Waldeck believed the Republic had the right to defend itself.

He first dissolved the Assumptionists, the most belligerent of the anti-
republican congregations and publisher of the violent daily *La Croix*. The
government then drafted and sought enactment of an Associations Act,
which required religious congregations to obtain state authorization from
France's highest administrative tribunal, the Council of State.

Waldeck campaigned for and defended the bill by pointing to the
profitable nonreligious activities carried out by many of the orders and,
more important, to the widespread extent of religious teaching unfriendly
to the Republic. He held that two types of youth, and thus two incompatible societies, were developing within France—one clerical, the other
lay. The strong act that was finally passed called not for a simple decree
but for a law of authorization and would therefore require parliamentary
debate. But the effect of the law would depend on the use made of it, and
that in turn depended on the outcome of the 1902 elections.

Radicals won definite control of the legislature and, by extension, of
future governments. Despite energetic Catholic support for conservative

candidates, the left added some thirty seats and could claim about 370; their opponents, claimed approximately 220. But before the new Chamber could meet, Waldeck suddenly announced his intention to resign on the grounds of ill health. No doubt he was suffering from the cancer that was to kill him in two years, but the prime minister resented the extreme radical complexion of the Chamber, and as he stated in his letter of resignation, he believed that "the Cabinet of 1899 no longer responded to the exigencies of the present situation."[2] Waldeck recommended as his successor the former seminary student turned doctor, minister of education, and president of the Senate committee that studied the associations bill, Emile Combes.

Combes was resolved to fight the "clerical devil" and enforce strict application of the new law. He was supported by a Radical Chamber, which, by creating the steering committee composed of representatives of the left-wing parties, ensured him a stable majority. Nonauthorized teaching orders were required to close their schools at once, while penalties for infringements of the law of 1901 were increased. Perhaps the most significant changes came in the procedures established to grant or deny authorization: the vote of either chamber, no longer one, was now considered sufficient. Numbers of congregations were collectively refused authorization, and by 1904 they could not engage in teaching of any kind.

Relations worsened between the Vatican and the French government. The exhausted Leo XIII had died in 1903, and his less subtle successor, Pius X, was determined to reassert the Church's independence of an anticlerical regime. Events followed each other quickly. President Loubet visited the king of Italy. The pope felt insulted (the newly established Italian kingdom had deprived the papacy of its temporal authority) and took no pains to conceal his displeasure from the heads of other European states. In reply, Combes recalled the French ambassador to the Vatican. Then, when Pius relieved two bishops of their duties without advising Paris, Combes expelled the papal nuncio and shortly after submitted legislation to abrogate the Concordat of 1801–1802.

That separation of church and state, by now inevitable, was best demonstrated by the fact that the necessary legislation came during the course of the relatively moderate Rouvier ministry. Its members wanted to move slowly, but in February 1905, the Chamber of Deputies, as recorded in its official journal, voted 338 to 185 that "the attitude of the Vatican renders separation necessary." A committee drafted a law to that effect, and the bill was guided through its many hearings by Aristide Briand, then a Socialist and a former spokesman for the general strike. Briand showed great ability to conciliate opposing views while urging enactment of the law in order that the country could "free itself from its veritable obsession" with the Church and turn to much-needed reform.

The Law of December 9, 1905, declared that the state recognized no religion but left the church its possessions and provided for voluntary associations to look after its interests. Despite a favorable response from a majority of French bishops, the Vatican condemned separation, and the papal encyclical *Vehementer Nos*, in February 1906, called it a "spoliation." Lay associations in particular were rejected as being opposed to the hierarchical principle embodied in the Roman Church. When the required inventory of Church possessions began, resistance was shown, a death resulted, and troops were called in. The attempt was halted by Clemenceau, minister of the interior in 1906, for whom "the counting of candles was not worth a soldier's life," and the problem would not be resolved until after World War I.[3]

Like others, university circles initially did not question Dreyfus's guilt, but it was in these circles, where it was customary to weigh evidence in support of conclusions, that large-scale doubt first arose. The Dreyfus Affair marked the first time that intellectuals as a group intervened in public life. The majority of professors who identified with the revisionist cause and signed petitions asking that the case be reopened had their classes disrupted and were shouted down; some were forced to resign. Anti-Dreyfusards held these intellectuals in contempt for daring to impugn the honor and wisdom of "men of action" and for meddling with matters outside the classroom. Not only did intellectuals provide leaders for the republican cause, but they derived support from the many school teachers, their former students, throughout France who were the most staunchly republican and most fiercely anticlerical contingent in the countryside. Ultimately, the intellectuals' extension of their criticism of Dreyfus's accusers to wide-ranging issues of social justice would turn numbers of them, most notably the novelist and future Nobel Prize winner, Anatole France, to Socialist causes.

Not only intellectuals but also other groups, in contrast to committees of notables, were making their presence felt: the extraparliamentary leagues, trade unions, cooperatives, women's organizations (such as the all-female Dreyfusard newspaper directed by Marguerite Durand and Socialist women's groups), and the press (which had turned the Dreyfus case into the Dreyfus Affair by amplifying, if not creating, public opinion and which had played a decisive role in both sending Dreyfus to prison and freeing him). These new groups, forces, and institutions were not created by the Dreyfus Affair, but the Affair immeasurably strengthened their influence. Because they had come to the defense of the Republic, Socialists and members of the labor force they claimed to represent were further integrated into the nation.

Anti-Semitism may have been continually condemned by various governments and the excesses carried out in its name were doubtless the work of an agitated minority, but few can deny the role of anti-Semitism in hardening animosities toward Dreyfus and (allied with nationalism) strengthening the resolve of anti-Dreyfusards. Thus, it comes as no surprise that a consequence of the Dreyfus Affair was the promotion of what historian Denis Bredin called a "Jewish specificity:" a quest for a Jewish national identity and the creation of organizations committed to achieving it. Bernard-Lazare's position evolved from that of an ardent advocate of Jewish assimilation to one of defense in a Jewish unity, and the journalist Theodor Herzl was finally convinced that only in a homeland of their own could Jews find security. Even so, Jewish integration into the larger society continued, and Zionism failed to win large numbers to its ranks. During the century that opened with Dreyfus's rehabilitation, the French would see several Jews serve as heads of government. The victory of the Dreyfusards did not bring an end to anti-Semitism, but it did discredit anti-Semitism on the left (an anti-Semitism that was not racially based but one that had identified Jews with the hated capitalist regime and had identified such personalities as Rothschild as the enemy).

Indeed, writers view the anti-Semitism and nationalist policies of the collaborationist Vichy regime as a "tragic sequel" to the Dreyfus Affair and as the "belated revenge" of the generals for their defeat. The general who allied himself with people sympathetic to Hitler's Germany, Marshal Philippe Pétain, did so out of an inbred defeatism. He also did so out of hatred for the Republic, like the generals at the time of the Affair. Where they failed, he thought he would succeed.[4] His ideology was nourished by his friend, the implacable anti-Dreyfusard Charles Maurras. The tragedy for France in 1940 lay in the absence of such men as Clemenceau,

Zola, or Jaurès who could fight against such reaction. Inasmuch as during the Vichy period (1940–1943) all anti-Dreyfusards defended—at least initially—the regime and all Dreyfusards opposed it, the old cleavages that distinguished the two camps endured well into the twentieth century. It is historical irony that the grandchildren of Alfred and Lucie Dreyfus were to die in the Holocaust, while the son of du Paty de Clam helped carry out those atrocities in his capacity as commissioner for Jewish matters.

On a broader canvas there is the conclusion, admittedly pessimistic, of the philosopher-historian Hannah Arendt who saw the vast concern with justice for an individual as belonging to the nineteenth century, to the dying world of the rights of man. She denotes the mob action, the anti-Semitic leagues, and the attempted coups as portents of twentieth-century totalitarianism struggling to be born.[5] She too believed that "what made France fall was the fact that she had no more true Dreyfusards," none who believed that democracy and freedom could any longer be defended under the Republic, so the Republic fell, "like overripe fruit into the lap of that old Anti-Dreyfusard clique which had always formed the kernel of her army." Pétainism did not grow out of German fascism, and this was made clear by its "slavish adherence" to the old formulas used forty years earlier by anti-Dreyfusards.[6]

Are the passions that animated the Dreyfus Affair still felt? Apparently in the upper ranks of the army they are. In 1994, on the hundredth anniversary of Dreyfus's arrest, the colonel who headed the army's historical service was fired by the defense minister for several errors made in his publication on the Affair and for implying that Dreyfus's innocence "is a thesis generally admitted by historians." The point is clear: after a hundred years, this officer could not bring himself uncategorically to declare Dreyfus innocent. Moreover, plans to hold a centenary exhibition at the Invalides (the military monument in Paris that contains Napoleon's tomb) raised objections from the military and threatened the exhibition. The following year, the new chief of the army's historical service officially declared Dreyfus innocent of all the charges raised against him in 1894, the first time that the army had done so, and the event was duly celebrated in such headlines as "Dreyfus Innocent—Official At Last." In 1998, on the hundredth anniversary of Zola's "J'accuse" letter, France's Roman Catholic daily paper, La Croix, apologized for its anti-Semitic articles published at the time of the Affair.

If the Dreyfus Affair is best understood as a product of the times in which it took place—the France of the 1890s and the social, cultural, and economic forces that confronted each other—it is also true that it pitted two attitudes, two moralities. The writer Maurice Barrès and the signers of the Henry monument evoked the nation, the army, honor, and God. Dreyfusards referred to the principles of justice and freedom that in their view transcended even the nation and the instrument designed to ensure its security, the army. If in the twentieth century it appeared that too often the former values triumphed (Vichy and the use of torture in the Algerian War to save the honor of the army, to cite two prominent examples), it is also true that the opposing forces, as they had in the 1890s, rallied in defense of *their* values: democracy and individual rights. The battle is perhaps eternal, to be refought every generation or two, and one can only hope that in the twenty-first century, the latter will continue to triumph. There are grounds for optimism. After all, the France that degraded Dreyfus in 1895, awarded him its Legion of Honor eleven years later, in the same place.

Notes

1. For the clearest statement of the latter view, see Rudolph Winnacher, "The Influence of the Dreyfus Affair on the Political Development of France," in *Papers of the Michigan Academy of Sciences, Arts, and Letters* 30 (1936): 465–478.

2. Waldeck-Rousseau Papers, Library of the French Institute, Box 4615.

3. David Robin Watson, *George Clemenceau: A Political Biography* (London: Eyre Metheun, 1974), 172.

4. Wilhelm Herzog, *From Dreyfus to Pétain: The Struggle of a Republic* (New York: Creative Age Press, 1947).

5. Hannah Arendt, *The Origins of Totalitarianism* (New York: Harcourt, Brace, 1951).

6. Arendt, 91–95.

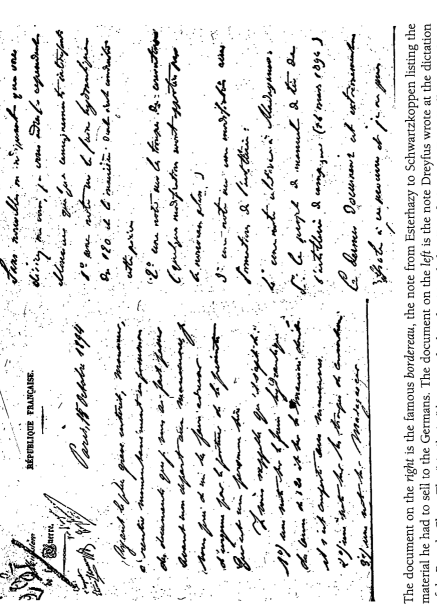

The document on the *right* is the famous *bordereau*, the note from Esterhazy to Schwartzkoppen listing the material he had to sell to the Germans. The document on the *left* is the note Dreyfus wrote at the dictation of du Paty de Clam. The "similarity" between the handwriting led to Dreyfus's arrest. From William Harding, *Dreyfus: The Prisoner of Devil's Island* (New York: Associated Publishing Co., 1899).

An artist's rendition of Dreyfus in his prison cell after his arrest but before the court-martial that would find him guilty of treason. He is being observed by the officer in the background, who is urging him to confess. From *Le Petit Journal*, Supplément Illustré, 20 January 1895.

Captain Alfred Dreyfus. This photograph was obviously taken before his arrest and deportation to Devil's Island. He appears young and energetic, in contrast to the aged officer who would return to France after almost five years' captivity. From William Harding, *Dreyfus: The Prisoner of Devil's Island* (New York: Associated Publishing Co., 1899).

The famous degradation ceremony. The sergeant-major has stripped
Dreyfus of his rank and is in the process of breaking his sword. A detachment of troops has been assembled to witness the event, and Dreyfus
will soon be forced to march before them, while shouting his innocence.
From *Le Petit Journal*, Supplément Illustré, 13 January 1895.

LEADING ACTORS IN THE DRAMA.

Colonel Henry.

Major Esterhazy.

M: Déroulède.

General Boisdeffre.

General Roget.

Four of the above, including Esterhazy, were army officers who preferred to have Dreyfus remain on Devil's Island. Paul Déroulède, in the upper-right-hand corner, was a fierce nationalist and outspoken anti-Dreyfusard. From William Harding, *Dreyfus: The Prisoner of Devil's Island* (New York: Associated Publishing Co., 1899).

LEADING ACTORS IN THE DRAMA.

Herr Schwarzkoppen,
Attaché of the German Embassy.

Signor Panizzardi,
Attaché of the Italian Embassy

M. Scheurer-Kestner,
Ex-Vice President of the Senate.

General Billot.

Colonel Sandherr.

Major Du Paty de Clam.

The two military attachés, Schwartzkoppen and Panizzardi, kept in close touch because of a personal relationship and because Germany and Italy were then allies. From William Harding, *Dreyfus: The Prisoner of Devil's Island* (New York: Associated Publishing Co., 1899).

THE GREAT ACTORS:

1. Zola.   2. Clemenceau.
3. Mercier.   4. Carrière.

Additional portraits of the leading personalities in the Dreyfus Affair. From William
Harding, *Dreyfus: The Prisoner of Devil's Island* (New York: Associated Publishing Co., 1899).

The front page of Georges Clemenceau's newspaper, *L'Aurore*, which carried Zola's famous letter to the president of the French Republic. Noticing the series of accusations at the end of the letter, Clemenceau suggested the title, *"J'accuse"* (I Accuse). The Marxist Socialist Jules Guesde called the letter and its publication "the most revolutionary act of the century." From *L'Aurore*, 13 January 1898.

L'AFFAIRE ZOLA

Zola au Palais de Justice

Zola is seen walking to the building where his trial is to take place. Note the crowd that has gathered, requiring the presence of police to keep order. From *Le Petit Journal*, Supplément Illustré, 15 February 1898

The most famous newspaper cartoon published during the Dreyfus Affair. The one on top shows a large family peacefully gathered at the dinner table. The caption reads, "Let's not speak of the Dreyfus Affair." The caption beneath the bottom cartoon (although it cannot be seen), reads simply, "They have spoken of it." The passions unleashed by the affair have separated families and friends. From *Le Figaro*, 13 February 1898.

Duels were still being fought at the end of the nineteenth century. Here Picquart is clashing swords with Henry, who had accused Picquart of fabricating the *petit-bleu* at the request of the Dreyfusards. When Henry was slightly wounded, Picquart regarded his honor as saved. From *Le Petit Journal*, Supplément Illustré, 20 March, 1898.

BIOGRAPHIES:
THE PERSONALITIES IN THE DREYFUS AFFAIR

Bernard-Lazare (1865–1903)

Bernard-Lazare was a young Jewish literary critic and journalist who early on embraced the Dreyfusard cause. He wrote the first pamphlet proclaiming Dreyfus's innocence and calling for revision.

Born Lazare Bernard into an "assimilated but observant" family in the southern French city of Nîmes, he left for Paris in 1886, where he began his postsecondary education. He then abandoned his religious beliefs (although not affiliation), quit his studies, transposed his name, and embarked on a literary career as an independent critic and poet. With a monocle, mustache, and goatee, Bernard-Lazare associated himself with the symbolist school of French poets (the Parnassien movement), which emphasized the intellectual and impersonal in contrast to lyrical romanticism. His political orientation corresponded to his literary outlook when he insisted on a social conscience for art and inveighed against the injustices of a heartless capitalism. He joined with anarchists—the philosophical and literary variety committed to social justice and not the political assassins and bomb throwers responsible for acts of terror. Bernard-Lazare and his friends founded a literary review to express their views, and by the age of thirty he was seen as a leading critic. In addition, he had responded to the anti-Semitic diatribes of Edouard Drumont in a well-received book, *Anti-Semitism: Its History and Its Causes*.

It was Bernard-Lazare's condemnation of anti-Semitism that led Mathieu Dreyfus to approach him. When Mathieu learned that his brother had been convicted on the strength of documents never shown to the defense because of alleged security concerns, he asked for Bernard-Lazare's help to keep the case in public view by encouraging newspapers to write stories about it. The latter was aware of the part played by anti-Semitism in the captain's arrest, but he initially brushed off Mathieu's request because he thought that if Dreyfus were innocent, his wealthy family would soon have the judgment reversed.

When the use of secret documents convinced Bernard-Lazare that Dreyfus had indeed fallen victim to prejudice, he joined forces with Mathieu. For a historian of the Affair and future prime minister of France, Léon Blum, he had become the "first" Dreyfusard (outside the family). At Mathieu's request and based on information he provided, Bernard-Lazare in 1896 wrote a pamphlet entitled, *A Judicial Error: The Truth about the Dreyfus Affair*. He also pressed the issue in the literary and political circles he frequented. However, Mathieu and Dreyfus's lawyer, Demange, believed that a family initiative at that time would not be helpful. They also rejected Bernard-Lazare's conviction that Judaism as a whole was being attacked through Dreyfus and his intention to wage war on the army and anti-Semitism rather than focus on the particulars of the case. To Bernard-Lazare's dismay, Mathieu urged that he delay publishing the pamphlet and wait for "a better opportunity." Bernard-Lazare criticized the traditional prudence shown by Jews as "a deplorable habit learned from old persecutions . . . not protesting . . . waiting for the storm to pass and playing dead so as not to attract the lightning." [1] Much of the Jewish community did not then support revision. They either believed that Dreyfus was guilty or did not want to give credence to charges that they were a nation within a nation.

A revised version of the pamphlet was published, first in Belgium and then by a sympathetic French firm, P.V. Stock, when details of the 1894 court-martial leaked to the press. Mathieu sent 3,000 copies to most French newspapers, politicians, army officers, and academics. Bernard-Lazare still insisted that Dreyfus's religion accounted for his arrest and conviction, but he placed greater emphasis on the irregularities surrounding his conviction. The pamphlet reproduced the exact words of the *bordereau*, the only document placed in evidence during the trial, and also described the divided opinions among the handwriting experts. Nevertheless, the pamphlet was largely ignored. Who would take the word of an anarchist and a Jew (Drumont said the author was paid to write by the Jews) over General Staff officers? Still, the important newspaper, *Le Matin*, on November 10, 1896, was prompted to publish a facsimile of the *bordereau.* Then in a second edition of his pamphlet, published in 1897, Bernard-Lazare defended Dreyfus in the name of the entire Jewish people, an approach not appreciated by the Dreyfusards, and cooperation between them diminished. In addition, Bernard-Lazare distributed posters that reproduced the *bordereau* and letters of Dreyfus placed side by side. It was one of Esterhazy's creditors who recognized the handwriting of the *bordereau* as that of his former client and accordingly informed Mathieu of it. Inasmuch as by the fall of 1897 Picquart had also identified Esterhazy as the author, revisionists both in and out of the army were fighting on two fronts to reopen the case.

Bernard-Lazare had also convinced the philosophy professor Lucien Lévy-Brühl of Dreyfus's innocence, and it was Lévy-Brühl who converted Lucien Herr, the thirty-three-year-old librarian of the prestigious *Ecole Normale*, a Socialist who had great influence on a younger generation of *Normaliens*. Lazare also shared information with Emile Zola in November 1897, which together with revelations from Picquart's lawyer brought the novelist into the Dreyfusard camp. Finally, at the time a pardon was debated, Bernard-Lazare urged Mathieu to persuade his brother to accept the government's offer.

Bernard-Lazare's broadside against anti-Semitism, set him apart from other Dreyfusards, but his role in 1895–1896 was crucial in keeping the case alive and opening the way to revision. His own political evolution was affected by the Affair. He originally favored Jewish assimilation into the larger society but was fully persuaded, particularly by the outcome of the Rennes court-martial, that Jews would never be totally accepted. His letter to Dreyfus, reproduced in the latter's memoirs, made it clear that the Affair was more than a legal mistake; it was the product of centuries of anti-Semitic prejudice. The 1899 court-martial sealed Bernard-Lazare's conversion to the cause of Jewish nationalism. Like Theodor Herzl, he became a Zionist. The first Zionist congress, held in Basel in 1897, adopted Bernard-Lazare's statement almost verbatim: "Assimilation is not and cannot be a solution."

Dreyfus, on the other hand, was convinced that Jewish emancipation had been achieved during the French Revolution. He experienced gratitude, not a sense of betrayal, toward the French state that had saved him from the consequences of a judicial error. He and most of those who rallied to his cause showed little interest in defending Jews in general. In a minority, silenced by the victorious Dreyfusards, the thirty-eight-year-old Bernard-Lazare died (of cancer) in obscurity in 1903.

Alphonse Bertillon (1853–1914)

Bertillon served as head of the criminal records office, known as the "anthropometric" or identification service, at the Paris Prefecture of Police. He testified at both the 1894 and 1899 courts-martial that Dreyfus had written the *bordereau*. Born in Paris, the son of one doctor and the brother of another, Bertillon was trained as an anthropologist. He won notoriety by inventing a system of identifying criminals that made use of anthropometry, that is, measuring certain parts of the body, for which he claimed infallibility. The parts included the length and breadth of the head, the length of the middle finger, the left foot, and the forearm to the tip of the middle finger. The need to make accurate measurements and the time required to do so made the process slow and expensive. (The use of fingerprint identification—and, now, DNA testing, which is replacing fingerprinting—rendered Bertillon's system obsolete.)

Bertillon also saw himself as a handwriting expert. After having Dreyfus arrested, his accusers called in a M. Gobert, the handwriting expert of the Bank of France, who said the *bordereau* might have been written by someone else. General Mercier, Major du Paty de Clam, and Lieutenant-Colonel Henry were left dissatisfied and called on Bertillon, a notorious anti-Semite. He reported that if no forgery was committed, then a comparison of handwritings showed that Dreyfus had to have written the *bordereau.*

As the Dreyfus case progressed, Bertillon maintained that the differences between the *bordereau* and Dreyfus's handwriting resulted from deliberate efforts made by the accused to alter the script and so disguise it. Bertillon claimed scientific accuracy for his methods, which provided "indisputable proof" of Dreyfus's guilt. When at the Rennes court-martial he brought as evidence hundreds of diagrams and enlarged photographs to defend the infallibility of his system, explained in arcane and convoluted language, the court exploded in laughter. His graphological theories were ridiculed by university mathematicians, and the president of the Republic, Casimir-Périer, called Bertillon "completely insane . . . a lunatic escaped from an asylum." This type of evidence was nevertheless relied on by the General Staff.

General Raoul de Boisdeffre (1839–1919)

This chief of staff of the army, acting on the orders of War Minister Mercier, ordered the arrest of Dreyfus. He testified against the accused before both military tribunals. Boisdeffre was born in Alençon (east of Paris) and in a lengthy military career saw service in Algeria and Russia. He became chief of staff in 1893.

Because Boisdeffre wrote a favorable performance report on Dreyfus after the latter began work on the General Staff in 1894, Dreyfus believed in his goodwill; he believed that Boisdeffre had fought for his release, and from Devil's Island, he asked his wife to solicit the general's help. It was in part his faith in Boisdeffre that led him to conclude that the high command had made an error but had not shown malice or prejudice. Even after learning of his superiors' manipulation of evidence, Dreyfus hoped that Boisdeffre was "not like the others," and on his return he tried to telegraph his appreciation for what he thought were the general's efforts on his behalf. Dreyfus was shattered when Boisdeffre testified in Rennes of his "absolute belief" in the condemned man's guilt.

After learning that Dreyfus was suspect, Boisdeffre asked his cousin, du Paty de Clam, an officer in the Statistical Section and an amateur handwriting expert, to join the investigation. When Picquart was appointed to head the Statistical Section, Boisdeffre urged him to look for additional evidence of Dreyfus's motives because "the Jews might mount an offensive" to free him. And Boisdeffre was one of Zola's "accused," along with Deputy Chief of Staff Gonse, of conspiring against Dreyfus, for Zola, "doubtless out of clerical passion." The Zola defense had asked that over 200 witnesses be called, including several generals. Terrified, Boisdeffre had tried to prevent the officers from appearing. He learned they were required to but could offer their testimony in secret, and Boisdeffre claimed their right to do so. He himself testified that Picquart had been "obsessed" by his belief in Esterhazy's guilt, had performed his duties poorly, and had been sent away on a legitimate assignment. Of Dreyfus's culpability, he was "absolutely certain." In closing, he told the jury, "You are the nation, and if the nation lacks confidence in its military leaders it should say so," and abruptly left the stand. To justify the refusal to produce a (forged) document, he threatened that war with Germany would follow.

Boisdeffre had guaranteed the authenticity of the forged letter, and he resigned immediately after Henry's confession. But because he (and

General Gonse) had kept in the background, they were left relatively untouched. Aside from his agreement to the use of a secret document in 1894 and his threat to resign in order to ensure Zola's conviction, there is no clear evidence of other crimes or improprieties. Some historians have found Boisdeffre (as well as Generals Gonse, Billot, and de Pellieux), in their attempts to protect the army—and admittedly, their own careers—more weak than culpable and have contrasted them with Henry and Mercier. Still, after having been told by Picquart that it was Esterhazy who wrote the *bordereau*, Boisdeffre prevented Picquart from continuing his investigation, sought to silence him, and so prevented the Affair from coming to an end in 1896.

Godefroy Cavaignac (1853–1905)

Cavaignac was minister of war for four months in 1898. Although an anti-Dreyfusard, his investigation of Colonel Henry led to the latter's confession of forgery and furthered the revisionist cause.

Cavaignac descended from a great republican family. His father had commanded the forces that suppressed the Paris workers' uprising in June 1848 and had been a candidate for the presidency of France's Second Republic. (He was defeated by Louis-Napoleon Bonaparte.) An uncle, whose own father had sat in the 1792–1794 Convention, participated in the Revolution of 1830 and was later jailed for his opposition to the July Monarchy. Cavaignac was a leader in the Radical party, and his anticlericalism and outspoken patriotism drew widespread admiration and reinforced his image as an ardent republican. Elected a deputy from Saint-Calais in 1882 and repeatedly reelected, he served as under-secretary of state for war in 1885, then as minister of war in 1895–1896, and in the same post from June to September 1898.

Cavaignac was an outspoken opponent of revision (and a cousin of du Paty de Clam). After Zola published his *"J'accuse"* letter, Cavaignac, as a Radical party spokesman, asked that a report on Dreyfus's alleged confession be made public. When Prime Minister Jules Méline, who had never seen the report, affirmed its reality, which implied that Dreyfus's confession was legitimate, Cavaignac withdrew his request to the applause of the Chamber.

The Méline ministry fell on June 15, 1898, not because of the Dreyfus Affair but because anticlerical Radicals were unhappy with the government's compromises with the Catholic right and Socialists rejected his conservative policies. Anti-Semites and nationalists also withheld support because they believed Méline was insufficiently critical of Dreyfus. They insisted that Cavaignac be named war minister in the Brisson ministry, which succeeded Méline's. Because of Cavaignac's presence, such anti-Dreyfusards as Paul Déroulède accepted the new government: Cavaignac would "safeguard the honor of the Army and the country."

In an important speech given July 7, 1898, Cavaignac, convinced of Dreyfus's guilt, stated that the army did not have to shelter behind security needs. The Dreyfusard Joseph Reinach, in his history of the Affair, described the sixty-two-year-old minister as "a well-educated moron who took himself completely at his own evaluation" and did so with "boundless self-confidence." Cavaignac convinced himself that he could settle the Dreyfus Affair by ousting the dissolute Esterhazy (for unprofessional conduct and for sending threats to President Faure) and demonstrating Dreyfus's guilt to the nation. He was sure that similarities between Esterhazy's writing and the *bordereau* showed that Esterhazy was Dreyfus's accomplice. Accordingly, he read to the Chamber of Deputies three "authentic" documents "proving" the captain's guilt. (Two turned out to be forgeries, most notably the note from the Italian military attaché Panizzardi to Schwartzkoppen where Henry changed the "P" to a "D," and a third was irrelevant.) By a 572 to 2 vote, the enthusiastic deputies, convinced the Dreyfus Affair was finally over, ordered the speech posted in all 36,000 communes of France.

The speech prompted Jaurès, who was aware of the forgeries, publicly to proclaim Dreyfus's innocence and begin publishing his *Les Preuves* (The Evidence). It also prompted Dreyfusard leaders to have Picquart, in an open letter to Cavaignac, argue that the documents were blatant forgeries. An outraged Cavaignac thereupon ordered Picquart's arrest for unprofessional conduct and for disclosing national security documents. But to place a final seal of approval on the authenticity of the Dreyfus dossier, he ordered a thorough review of it. It was this review that revealed the forgery committed by Henry.

On August 30 Cavaignac ordered Henry, now a lieutenant-colonel, to his office and in the presence of Generals de Boisdeffre, Gonse, and Roget, interrogated him aggressively. Cavaignac pointed to similarities in the two relevant documents and insisted they had been changed. He advised Henry to confess inasmuch as no explanation would be as damning as an inadequate one. Hammering away at him, Cavaignac finally forced Henry to admit that what he had done was for the good of the country. When he still refused to acknowledge forgery, Cavaignac said, "Tell it all! You got a letter of no consequence in 1896. You buried it and forged another." Cornered and exhausted, Henry finally said, "Yes."

Even after Henry's confession and suicide, Cavaignac continued to insist on Dreyfus's guilt. The Henry forgery, he argued, dated from 1896 and so had nothing to do with the *bordereau*—remarks that reassured the generals. He denied that revision was inevitable when this was suggested by another cabinet member. He told fellow Radical and former Prime Minister Léon Bourgeois, who tried to reason with him, that he would arraign all the Dreyfusards before the High Court. Bourgeois concluded that he was mad. Finally, Cavaignac resigned. Instead of bringing the Affair to an end, as he had hoped, he had done the opposite: Henry was shown to be a forger, Esterhazy had fled, he himself had resigned, and the public had accepted the need to reopen the case.

Cavaignac later joined the anti-Dreyfusard Ligue de la Patrie Française (League of the French Fatherland) and signed its manifesto. He led the anti-Dreyfusard campaign to transfer the case from the Criminal Chamber of the High Court in late 1898 (presided over by a Jew and accordingly denounced as corrupt) to the court in its entirety. Actually, Dreyfusards agreed that given the furor of the antirevisionist press, in so momentous a proceeding responsibility should be that of the entire court. Appropriate legislation to "dispossess" the Criminal Chamber of the case was passed in February 1899. Ironically, the antirevisionists' struggle persuaded many hitherto moderates that nationalists and anti-Semites threatened the very existence of the Republic. Finally, the unrepentant Cavaignac testified on behalf of the prosecution against Dreyfus at the Rennes courtmartial.

Georges Clemenceau (1841–1929)

Clemenceau became an ardent Dreyfusard who believed in the innocence of the accused. He also seized the opportunity to pursue an anticlerical and staunchly republican agenda. Clemenceau's career almost spanned that of France's Third Republic. After he completed his medical studies in 1865, he gravitated to opponents of the Second Empire. Elected a deputy in 1871, he objected to the peace preliminaries with Prussia, and as mayor of Montmartre (not yet incorporated into a larger Paris) he sympathized with the insurrection known as the Paris Commune. As a leading Radical (then progressive) member of parliament in the 1880s, he fought the corrupt, conservative, and imperialist policies of the more Opportunist (i.e., moderate republican) governments, and his forceful speeches brought about the downfall of several of them. At that time, Clemenceau favored constitutional revision and economic and social reform. Although he initially supported General Georges Boulanger, he was soon converted to a strong advocacy of republican defense when the ambitious general showed signs of authoritarianism. His career seemed at end when he was (unjustly) accused of complicity in the Panama scandal in the early 1890s. Having lost his seat in the Chamber, he turned to journalism.

Once persuaded of Dreyfus's innocence, Clemenceau saw the Affair as symbolizing the struggle of the innocent victim against the forces of tyranny and dogma, that is, against the army and the Church. As the political editor of the newspaper *L'Aurore* (The Dawn), he fiercely defended Dreyfus in numerous articles, published Zola's "*J'accuse*" letter (suggesting the title), and had to be persuaded of the necessity of Dreyfus's pardon. A pardon, Clemenceau had believed, implied an admission of guilt. As prime minister after 1906, he became an ardent defender (France's "first cop") of the established social order (with Jaurès as his arch-enemy) when his government severely and repeatedly suppressed workers' strikes in Paris and throughout the country. A critic of early governments during World War I for failing to pursue the war effort more vigorously, Clemenceau formed a government of his own in 1917 that subordinated every policy decision to the need to win the war—and won him the nickname "The Tiger" and acclaim as the "Father of Victory." His leading role at the Paris Peace Conference is well known. Denied the presidency of the Republic because conservatives resented his fierce anticlericalism, Clemenceau criticized what he saw as appeasement of Germany in the last years of his life.

At first, Clemenceau had not questioned Dreyfus's guilt ("How could a man carry out such an act?"), but was persuaded by Scheurer-Kestner and Arthur Ranc (a left-wing Radical, then a senator, and a longtime associate of Clemenceau), if not of the condemned man's innocence at least of the irregularities in the trial. His revisionist articles in *L'Aurore* were motivated by both the wish to bring down the government and to secure justice, and in seeking to reopen the case, Clemenceau became a close collaborator of Mathieu Dreyfus. When at the time of the Esterhazy trial twelve hundred "writers, artists, and academics" who had joined the Dreyfusard cause signed a petition demanding that the case be reopened, Clemenceau called it the "Manifesto of the Intellectuals," defining *intellectuals* as a politically committed elite and giving the term its modern meaning. After the Zola trial, together with other Dreyfusard leaders, Clemenceau persuaded the novelist that he would be more useful abroad than stagnating in a prison cell. Clemenceau was critical of President Faure for failing to side with the revisionists and after Faure's death stated that he would support the candidacy of Emile Loubet, who was known to favor revision. When on July 7, 1898, Cavaignac made his famous speech affirming Dreyfus's guilt, Clemenceau declared that because the minister read documents never shown to the defense at the time of the court-martial, he had made a review of the case inevitable.

Following the Rennes verdict and in view of his brother's failing health—and convinced that no further appeal could succeed—Mathieu Dreyfus sought a presidential pardon. Clemenceau and Jaurès, however, saw a pardon as equivalent to an admittance of guilt. The Affair, they believed, transcended the victim, and a pardon would deprive the Dreyfusards of a martyr and so bring an end to its heroic phase. "After a whole people has been roused to fight for justice," they argued, "they are supposed to be satisfied with a pardon for a single individual?" For Clemenceau, only full rehabilitation for Dreyfus would be just revenge on the militarists and clericals he had fought all his life. But when Mathieu insisted on unanimity in agreeing to the offer of a pardon, Clemenceau reluctantly agreed: "If I were his brother, I would accept," he said.[2] What Clemenceau and the others found most upsetting was the Waldeck-Rousseau government's success in enacting an amnesty, which became law in late 1900 and prevented future proceedings against any of the officers responsible for creating and continuing the Affair but allowing Dreyfus (from a legal standpoint) to remain a traitor and excluding him and Picquart from the army.

Edgar Demange (1841–1925)

Demange served as Dreyfus's lawyer in both the 1894 and 1899 courts-martial and also represented Mathieu Dreyfus when he filed a civil suit against Esterhazy in hopes of exposing his treason. Aside from the Dreyfus family (and the prison warden Forzinetti), Demange was the first to believe in Dreyfus's innocence and he remained a staunch supporter and friend of the family.

Edgar Demange was born in Versailles. He studied law and was the defense lawyer in several notorious trials, including that of a Bonaparte prince who murdered a journalist, and in one way or another he participated in many of the great affairs in the early Third Republic. As a fervent Catholic and admirer of the army, he had represented an outspoken anti-Semite accused of killing a Jewish officer in a duel. Thus, Demange seemed an unlikely choice to defend Dreyfus. On the other hand, his religion, conservatism, and past record would shield him from the bitterest anti-Dreyfusard invective. The fifty-three-year-old attorney was a thorough professional who had earned his reputation in difficult defense cases. He agreed to Mathieu's request on the condition that his own examination of the dossier must convince him of the accused's innocence. After the examination, a shaken Demange concluded that "if Captain Dreyfus were not Jewish, he would not be in [Cherche-Midi] prison" and that to indict him on such flimsy evidence was "an abomination."[3] He would provide constant moral as well as legal support for Dreyfus and his family, become a close friend of Mathieu, and break down on hearing the guilty verdict rendered by the Rennes court-martial.

It was at the Rennes trial that Demange's cautious approach and insistence on showing respect for military authority clashed with that of his younger colleague, Fernand Labori, who was more passionate, theatrical, and outwardly hostile. Labori, who had participated in some sensational trials, had previously collaborated with Demange: he had represented Lucie Dreyfus at the Esterhazy court-martial (Demange had represented Mathieu) and together with Clemenceau's brother and Clemenceau himself, had defended Zola. Thus, Labori was retained by the Dreyfus family to work with Demange in bringing Dreyfus, newly returned from Devil's Island, up to date. The two lawyers brought stacks of documents, and as related in his memoirs Dreyfus had "listened breathlessly [to] the long series of misdeeds, villainies and crimes" that secured his conviction.

At Rennes, Demange was critical of Labori's impassioned rhetoric and melodramatic gestures, which he felt were scarcely suited to a military tribunal. The two fought over the strategy to be taken by the defense:

Demange was concerned with proving Dreyfus innocent and not with finding the General Staff guilty. Mathieu had to intervene. He appreciated
Labori's determination—at the very real risk of his life in view of the attempt to assassinate him—to uncover the corruption of the military high
command and to defend the Republic but preferred that the closing remarks be made by Demange. Demange shared the family's belief in the
need to maintain respect for French justice and for five years devoted himself to the Dreyfusard cause. In his five-hour summation, he delivered the
"judicious exposition" favored by Mathieu. In contrast to Labori's histri-
onics, he spoke calmly and never appeared to question the good faith of
the military judges. His aim was to raise doubt by minutely examining
every piece of evidence, for that would mean acquittal. Later, the two
lawyers also disagreed over the proposed pardon: Labori sided with
Clemenceau and Picquart in wishing to reject it and accused Demange of
yielding to Waldeck-Rousseau's political imperatives.

   In the years that followed, Demange continued to take up unpopular causes. In 1919, he defended the Radical deputy Joseph Caillaux, who
in World War I had wanted to negotiate a peace with Germany and had
been charged with working with the enemy. Ironically, this defense openly
pitted him against his former ally in the Dreyfus Affair, Prime Minister
Clemenceau. (Caillaux was sentenced to a three-year prison term but was
later amnestied and able to reenter a government.) After his retirement,
Demange continued to frequent the Palais de Justice (the cluster of law
courts in the center of Paris) and, appropriate for a devout Catholic, to
reside, until his death in 1925 at eighty-four years of age, in the shadow
of the Notre Dame cathedral.

Alfred Dreyfus (1859–1935)

   Ironically, the most poorly informed participant in much of the
Dreyfus Affair—certainly from the time of his deportation on February 22,
1895, until his return to France June 30, 1899—was the victim himself,
Alfred Dreyfus. He then had to be briefed by his brother and his lawyers
about the "evidence" used to convict him and about the growing number
of supporters who had rallied to his cause.

   Alfred Dreyfus was born into a financially comfortable Jewish family
of textile manufacturers in Alsace, the French province that was incorporated into the new German Empire after the Franco-Prussian War of 1870–

1871. As an eleven-year-old boy, he experienced his "first sadness" on seeing German troops march into his home city of Mulhouse, an important industrial center, and his resentment of the Germans influenced his choice of a military career. Aside from one brother, designated to stay behind in Alsace and manage the family enterprise, the family chose to remain French and relocate to Paris. To further the process of acculturation, the spelling of the family name was changed from Dreyfuss to Dreyfus. The youngest of seven children (three sisters and three brothers), Alfred was closest to his brother Mathieu, who became something of a model for him. A shy, nearsighted, intense boy, poor at games but good with books and excellent in math, he contrasted with the outgoing, athletic Mathieu.

Alfred received an excellent education in preparatory school and in 1876 passed the difficult examination for the *baccalauréat* (the degree awarded by examination at the conclusion of secondary school studies and required for entry to universities). Two years later, he was admitted to the Ecole Polytechnique, one of France's prestigious establishments of higher learning. He graduated high in his class and shortly afterward entered the army as a second lieutenant. He spent the next ten years in training as an artillery officer. He performed exceptionally well and by the age of thirty-four was already a captain and General Staff probationer. The future looked bright; his hope of reaching the rank of general did not seem unreasonable. He had married Lucie Hadamard, the daughter of a wealthy Paris diamond merchant, fathered two children, and lived with his family in the smart Sixteenth Arrondissement of Paris.

His personal evaluations showed the young officer as "intelligent," "knowledgeable and always learning," "hard-working," and "conscientious." His brother Mathieu described him as extremely patriotic, happy, and "proud to wear his uniform." However, a lack of humor, a stiffness, an unemotional demeanor, an apparent arrogance, and his religion kept him apart from his fellow officers.

Dreyfus was admitted to the War College in 1890, whose top graduates could expect assignment to the General Staff. No acknowledged Jew, however, had ever served on the General Staff. Moreover, mounting anti-Semitic agitation dimmed his prospects for a successful career. The first anti-Semitic newspaper had appeared in 1871 following the collapse of a Catholic financial giant, the Union Générale bank—a collapse ascribed to the machinations of a Jewish financial "syndicate." The influx of thousands of Eastern European Jews fleeing persecution led to fears that French workers would lose their jobs, and particularly disturbing articles were published in a popular anti-Semitic newspaper, *La Libre Parole*, on Jewish "infiltration" of the army. Self-confident, apolitical, and religious in name only, Dreyfus brushed aside these developments.

He graduated ninth in his class. It would have been higher if not for the evaluation of an anti-Semitic general who said it would be "unwise" to have a Jew assigned to the General Staff. (Dreyfus's superiors admitted the unfairness of the evaluation but maintained they were powerless to override the views of a general.) He was nevertheless appointed. Officers on the General Staff, including Majors Georges Picquart and Armand du Paty de Clam, regretted the designation of a Jewish colleague; others who were critical of his wealth, his conceit, and his religion concurred. They could scarcely conceal their envy of his expertise, particularly when, on maneuvers, the chief of staff, Lieutenant-General Boisdeffre, paid close attention to Dreyfus's views on artillery matters, even inviting the young trainee to accompany him on a walk. Boisdeffre's interest and amiability helped to persuade Dreyfus that the highest authorities would soon correct the "error" that had led to his arrest, conviction, and sentence to life imprisonment.

After the discovery of the *bordereau*, Dreyfus was accused, tried, and convicted for treason. On the voyage to French Guiana, totally unaware of his destination, he was kept manacled in an iron cage, watched by guards day and night. He was transferred from the main penal colony off the coast to the outlying Isle du Diable (Devil's Island), which had been cleared of the lepers who previously lived there. He was the solitary prisoner there, kept under twenty-four-hour surveillance. He lived in a stone hut with a corrugated metal roof. Another hut housed his five guards (frequently rotated because of illness) and their superior. There was no privacy; every two hours with the change of guard, lantern light flooded Dreyfus's hut making continuous sleep impossible. For sanitation, a waste bucket sat next to his cot.

With a wholly inadequate diet and only fetid water to drink, Dreyfus suffered from chronic dysentery and bouts of malaria. Wild goats had provided fresh milk for the lepers, but fearing that he might take hold of one and swim out to sea, his guards removed them. Sharks would have torn both to pieces, but the authorities were to take no chances. Malnutrition and illness took their toll. During his four and a half years on the island, his body shriveled, his hair thinned, and his teeth loosened. Aside from medical attention, he lived, according to his memoirs, in "profound, eternal, and tortuous silence." Dreyfus found the heat intolerable, especially when he was locked in the stifling hut after 6:00 P.M. When false rumors of his escape surfaced, he was confined to the hut during the day, and at night his feet were chained to the bed in a sort of pillory, rendering him immobile and exposed to the crabs, mosquitoes, and ants crawling to his body. He endured this additional punishment for forty days.

His only solace and only consolation was the diary he kept and the letters he wrote to, and twice a month received from, his family, especially his wife, who wrote every day. He could not understand what was happening to him or why. "How can it be said," Dreyfus wrote in his diary, "that in our century and in a country like France, imbued with the ideas of justice and truth, something as fundamentally unjust as this can happen?"

Because the letters from Lucie, his wife, were censored, he knew nothing of the events that had made his arrest a cause célèbre. He insisted that unscrupulous individuals, and not his beloved army, had been at fault and that once the truth was known, matters would be set right. After his return and second conviction by a military tribunal, he had to be persuaded by Mathieu and his wife to accept the pardon because of poor health.

Not until July 12, 1906, did a united High Court annul the Rennes verdict, unanimously find Dreyfus innocent of all charges, and by a majority vote decide against referring the case to yet another military court. Twenty-four hours later, the government asked for legislation reintegrating both him and Picquart into the army, with the ranks of major and brigadier general, respectively.

But even here Dreyfus suffered discrimination (this time by a Dreyfusard government), doubtless for the allegedly unheroic role played in accepting the pardon. While Picquart was given seniority for the time spent as a civilian, Dreyfus was not and so was denied higher promotion. Fears that the military would tolerate no higher rank for the officer whose arrest had humiliated them may have contributed to the decision not to advance his rank. Still, he was inducted into the Legion of Honor on July

20, before his retirement the following year. With the outbreak of war in 1914, he returned to active duty as a lieutenant-colonel and then permanently retired at the war's end with the rank of colonel.

In the remaining decade and a half of his life, Dreyfus never accepted the role of a Dreyfusard, even insisting that he was an artillery officer whose career had been interrupted by a tragic mistake and denying that he was a "symbol of justice." Only once did he play that part: in August 1927, he appealed to the state of Massachusetts to spare the lives of two convicted anarchists, Sacco and Vanzetti, but to no avail. After a long illness, Dreyfus died on July 12, 1935, forty years and three months after his arrival on Devil's Island.

Mathieu Dreyfus (1857–1930)

Mathieu, the brother closest to Alfred Dreyfus, worked tirelessly to have the case reopened. More than anyone else, he was responsible for Dreyfus's retrial, restoration to freedom, and ultimate exoneration, tasks to which he devoted his life for five years. He used every weapon available, and in so doing, his unending efforts made anti-Dreyfusards speak of a "Jewish syndicate" with unlimited financial resources to bribe clerks, give false stories to the press, and leak court documents.

Mathieu and Alfred were the youngest of seven children and unlike the others took French as their mother tongue, even in German-speaking Alsace. Like Alfred, Mathieu was educated in Paris, but he planned to follow his two older brothers in the family textile business. A liberal republican, he wanted to see separation of church and state and would become a Freemason. After the death of their father in 1893, Matheiu became the manager of the family's holdings and worked to expand the business. Four years earlier, the thirty-one-year-old Mathieu had married Suzanne Schwab, the twenty-year-old daughter of a wealthy textile manufacturer, in a civil ceremony. They remained in Mulhouse, the only Alsatian city in the new German Empire where the French language thrived, thanks to fiercely patriotic families like the Dreyfuses.

It was Mathieu who rushed to Paris on October 31, 1894, in response to Lucie Dreyfus's frantic telegram announcing her husband's arrest. He retained the lawyer Demange and would work tirelessly to have his brother cleared. He told the family not to stay discouraged while he lined up character witnesses for the 1894 court-martial. He paid for the copying of legal briefs (and so first saw the *bordereau* and how flimsy the army's case was) and after the guilty verdict, promised Lucie he would remain in Paris "to search for the truth." He tried everything, from hiring detectives to meeting with a psychic and speaking with the president of the Republic, numerous politicians, and newspaper editors, fully aware of how much his brother depended on him for his freedom.

To break public indifference, he spread the rumor that Alfred had escaped from Devil's Island. He drafted petitions to have the case reopened. For Mathieu and the rest of the family, the arrest was "a tragic error" by misguided individuals or criminals, not a failure of French justice. He hired the young writer Bernard-Lazare who, once familiar with the documents, published brochures and pamphlets refuting the charges. He paid for posters contrasting the handwriting of the *bordereau* (which had been published by the Paris newspaper *Le Matin*) and that of his brother; and when he realized that Esterhazy was the real author, he approached Senator Scheurer-Kestner. Because of Picquart's effort, the senator already knew of Esterhazy's guilt but had been honor bound not to divulge it.

After Alfred's return to France to stand trial again, Mathieu joined with Demange and Labori to bring his brother up-to-date on all that had transpired since the arrest and to tell him of the new allies won to his cause. When Scheurer-Kestner identified Esterhazy as the traitor, and on the advice of Louis Leblois (Picquart's lawyer), Mathieu formally accused the dissolute officer of having written the *bordereau*. Esterhazy insisted on a court-martial "to clear his name," and it convened on November 15, 1897. All of these activities led to Mathieu's condemnation by anti-Dreyfusards as the "crafty Jew" and the leader of the "Jewish syndicate." Police protection was required for both brothers and their families. Mathieu played a key role in securing a presidential pardon and acting as a mediator between the two defense lawyers. Mathieu had finally persuaded his brother, who "thirsted for justice," to accept the pardon, although he found the amnesty that permitted Mercier and his co-conspirators to escape punishment "shameful" and "wretched."

Later in his life, Mathieu supported the decision of his son, Emile, to embark on a military career. The Dreyfus name, he believed, carried a special obligation to show the army and the nation as once more united. Struck by shrapnel in the fighting of World War I, Emile died in October 1915.

Distraught by his workers' demands, which he and an older generation of industrialists regarded as unpatriotic and after consulting with Alfred and his sisters, Mathieu sold the family textile complex and devoted his energies to helping raise his grandchildren. He published his memoirs of the Affair, which echoed his belief that weak and bigoted individuals, not French institutions, were responsible for the injustices committed. After suffering a stroke and surrounded by his family, Mathieu Dreyfus died in his home in Paris on October 22, 1930. In a whispered good-bye close to the coffin, Alfred was heard to say, "I owe you everything."

Edouard Drumont (1844–1917)

More a polemicist than a newspaperman, Drumont did much to invigorate anti-Semitism in France. He founded the *Ligue Antisémetique* (Anti-Semitic League), and it was his newspaper, *La Libre Parole*, that broke the story of an officer arrested for selling military secrets and put pressure on the army to find a culprit. Drumont represented the extremist wing of the anti-Dreyfusard movement and encouraged agitation and street violence. A bitter, violent man with bushy black hair, Drumont was a fanatic who shrewdly pitched his appeal to large audiences, making use of a vague populism, a fervent nationalism, religious belief, and a harsh determinism. ("The Jew, being what he is, cannot act otherwise.") Throughout the course of the Dreyfus Affair, he repeatedly assured his readers of the accused's "absolute guilt" and of the existence of a Dreyfusard "syndicate"— traitors supplied with Jewish money setting out to destroy France.

The political and social climate provided the combustible material for an anti-Semitic outburst. The French defeat at the hands of the "barbarians from across the Rhine" led to cries of traitors who were betraying the fatherland. The arrival of Jewish refugees fleeing persecution and the financial scandals associated with the failed attempt to build a Panama Canal also contributed to a wave of anti-Semitism when the names of some prominent Jewish politicians and financiers surfaced. All that was needed was a spark, and Drumont provided it.

Of peasant origins, he first worked at the Seine Prefecture but left the civil service to become a writer and journalist. In 1886, Drumont published his two-volume *La France juive* (Jewish France) attacking Jewish financiers and resurrecting medieval anti-Semitic legends. The book proved immensely popular: there were 150 printings in France, and so ardent was Drumont's belief in his message that he sold the Spanish rights for an absurdly low sum and gave the Polish rights away. There was a German edition as well. The twelve-hundred-page book tried to show that Jews and their "hirelings" could give allegiance only to "the Promised Land of Israel," that they constituted "a nation within a nation," and could never be true citizens. They had been responsible for every disaster and humiliation suffered by France. Drumont contrasted the "business-like, greedy, intriguing, subtle, and crafty" Semite with the "enthusiastic, heroic, chivalric, disinterested, and open" Aryan.[4] Even assimilated Jews belonged to the same "foreign tribe," disregarding the French Jews who had fought in Napoleon's armies and in subsequent wars, and the hundreds then serving loyally in the army. Drumont denied any personal animosity: again, the Jews could not help being Jews; they should just go somewhere else.[5]

In April 1892 Drumont launched his newspaper, *La Libre Parole*, subtitled *"La France au français"* (France for the French), and because of revelations of widespread corruption in the Panama Affair, it rapidly achieved a circulation of 200,000 copies. He at once published a series of articles claiming to expose "Jewish contamination of the military." It is true that the number of Jews in the military was increasing, but Drumont saw this as infiltration, not patriotism. The articles were most likely read by such anti-Semitic officers as Major Georges Picquart, who assigned Dreyfus tasks unrelated to national security, and Lieutenant-Colonel Joseph Henry of the counterintelligence branch, and his superior, Colonel Jean-Conrad Sandherr, who had refused to have Dreyfus assigned to his service.

When on October 31, 1894, news broke that an officer on the General Staff had been arrested, General Mercier, the war minister, confirmed the story. But to protect himself, he minimized the event and did not mention Dreyfus by name. The next morning, *La Libre Parole* printed a long front-page article under the sensational headline, "High Treason: The Jewish Traitor Alfred Dreyfus Arrested." In the weekly illustrated edition of the newspaper published on November 3, Drumont reminded readers that "with regard to the Judas Dreyfus, Frenchmen, for eight years I have been warning you every day." Other newspapers picked up the story and reproduced Drumont's inaccurate rendition of events: that Dreyfus had confessed and that Germany was involved. The anti-Semitic campaign against Dreyfus was thus unleashed.

Drumont hoped that by exploiting the case, he would further the anti-Semitic cause by making it a political movement. Despite his best efforts, he had not been able to make much progress, and because he had earlier fled to Belgium to avoid litigation in a contempt case, he had lost popularity. Dreyfus's arrest provided an opportunity for a fresh start. In article after article, Drumont denounced Mercier for moving too slowly. Was it because of "Jewish pressure"? When would a trial begin? When Mercier made use of a secret file, Drumont's criticisms overnight turned to congratulations.

At each stage of the Dreyfus Affair, Drumont responded to new allegations. The December 27, 1894, issue of *La Libre Parole* suggested that Germany erect a statue to the spy from Alsace. On news of the guilty verdict, the newspaper's banner headline repeated its subtitle, France for the French. It rejected charges of poor treatment of the prisoner on Devil's Island and described Dreyfus as living comfortably. When Mathieu spread false rumors of his brother's escape, Drumont unblushingly published a fabricated interview with the captain of the ship that supposedly took him to freedom. When all this was exposed as never having taken place, Drumont's readers chuckled at his nerve. At the time of Zola's letter accusing the army chiefs of conspiracy, Drumont and his friends responded in an open letter of their own to President Faure denouncing the Dreyfusard Joseph Reinach. *La Libre Parole* circulated a story that Bernard-Lazare had been paid 5,000 francs by the Dreyfus family to discredit the army and the nation, and the newspaper carried anti-Semitic agitator Jules Guérin's denunciation of "the Jewish syndicate." Drumont had earlier accused Zola of accepting "Jewish money," and his contempt for the novelist knew no limits. "That son of an Italian immigrant" had revealed his true character as "the falsest, most declamatory, most verbose, windiest of all writers."[6] The night before the Zola trial opened, posters appeared on Paris streets with the signatures of Drumont and others threatening "agents of foreign countries" and promising that order would be kept by "patriotic Parisians" serving as police. *La Libre Parole* greeted the outcome of the Rennes trial as "a beautiful spectacle," and when anti-Dreyfusards questioned the competency of the high court's Criminal Chamber (it was presided over by a Jewish judge), the newspaper published his name and address as well as those of the associate judges, and asked its readers, "What precious lives are sheltered at these mysterious locations?"[7]

After one of Drumont's more acerbic articles, Clemenceau challenged him to a duel. Six shots were fired without result. Nationalists and anti-Semites were determined to take advantage of the national legislative elections in 1898. Fifteen of the fiercest anti-Dreyfusards—including Drumont, who ran as a candidate from Algiers, Paul Déroulède, and Paul de Cassagnac—were elected. They took seats on the far right of the new Chamber, which epitomized the movement of nationalism in France from the left to the right.

The disclosure of Henry's forgery left Drumont in a quandary. He described it as "idiotic" but remained confident even in the event the case was reopened. When Reinach said that Henry had worked with Esterhazy, the December 14, 1899, issue of *La Libre Parole* initiated an appeal to cover the costs of the libel suit that Henry's widow was bringing against Reinach, an appeal for funds to rehabilitate the "victim of duty." A banner was draped over the balcony of the newspaper's offices with the words: "For the widow and orphan of Colonel Henry. Against the Jew Reinach." When President Faure was found dead (of a heart attack while entertaining his mistress), Drumont took advantage of rumors about the deceased's amorous exploits to talk of the murder committed by the "Dreyfusard Delilah."

With the guilty verdict against Déroulède and his associates for the coup attempted at the end of 1899 (he was sentenced to ten years of exile), Drumont began to lose influence. The anti-Semitic cause could no longer be fought under its own flag; it had to be fought under that of others when in July 1906 the High Court quashed the guilty verdict. Drumont, Rochefort, Barrés, and other anti-Dreyfusards bewailed the decision, but few people paid much attention. Drumont had tied himself so close to the losing cause and had lost so much influence that he died in poverty and obscurity in 1917.

His cause did not. During World War II, Vichy officials pursued anti-Semitic policies. Jews were again seen as "undesirable aliens." The head of the new Commissariat for Jewish Affairs, Darquier de Pellepoix, who called for "cleaning up Jewish scum" as a necessary step to ensure "public hygiene," proudly evoked "first-rate men" like Drumont as his predecessors. And in February 1942 the Association of Anti-Jewish Journalists placed flowers on the grave of their "great colleague Drumont, who had lashed out against the first wave of Jewish power."[8]

Marie Charles Ferdinand Walsin Esterhazy (1847–1923)

Esterhazy sold military secrets to the Germans, the crime for which Dreyfus was convicted. A French infantry officer attached to the General Staff, he demanded a court-martial when named as the culprit, and with the support of his superiors he was acquitted.

Although born in Paris, Esterhazy was the grandson of an illegitimate member of a noble Hungarian family that dated from the time of the Holy Roman Empire and had owned huge tracts of land. A branch of the family had emigrated to France in the late eighteenth century. His father was a general who died ten years after his son's birth.

Unable to secure the coveted *baccalauréat*, Esterhazy also failed the entrance examination for Saint-Cyr, France's equivalent of West Point. Rather than enter the army as an enlisted man, he joined the "legion" that guarded the papal estates in the newly created Kingdom of Italy. He became an officer and then, because of the intervention of his uncle, another general, transferred to the French Foreign Legion. Esterhazy saw action in the Franco-Prussian War of 1870–1871, and was given a permanent commission in the regular army. Thanks to a small inheritance, he lived the life of a dissolute officer: gambling, chasing women, and falling into debt. He possessed an easy charm that won him contacts with politicians, journalists, and his superiors, and few questioned him when he began calling himself a "count." After the intervention of an actress, he was posted to the Statistical Section, where he met Captain Henry. Suffering from tuberculosis and the demands of unhappy creditors, Esterhazy sought a command in the drier—and more distant—climate of North Africa. He had access to his unit's records and having glorified his role in battle had himself transferred back to Paris, although, again, strings had to be pulled, this time by a mistress and a relative.

By 1886, he had gambled away his inheritance. The thirty-nine-year-old Esterhazy then married twenty-two-year-old Anne de Nettancourt, daughter of an aristocratic family, but he was unable to touch much of her large dowry when she finally put a stop to his withdrawals from their joint bank account. Now a major, unhappily married and debt ridden, Esterhazy approached the German military attaché with an offer to sell secrets for cash. After initially hesitating, fearing Esterhazy might be a double agent, Schwartzkopppen received orders from Berlin to accept. Esterhazy's decision to betray his country also came in the context of his contempt for his superiors. "The French have not understood me," he would write later, "so much the worse for them."[9] Esterhazy asked the Germans for a salary, not payment based on the value of the intelligence provided. Ultimately, he agreed that payment would hinge on the quality of the first deliveries. Several were made. When told that Berlin wanted even more important information, Esterhazy compiled some documents and sent a covering note—the famous *bordereau*—describing them to Schwartzkoppen. That was the (torn) note found by the French cleaning woman that set the Dreyfus Affair in motion.

When Picquart's comparison of the *petit-bleu*'s and Esterhazy's hand-writing convinced him that it was Esterhazy and not Dreyfus who wrote the *bordereau*, when Mathieu independently reached the same conclusion, and after the case had flared up because of the revelation that secret evidence had been shown to the military tribunal, Esterhazy brazenly decided to bluff. He had not been arrested (he had well-placed friends and he was not a Jew), and he openly sought promotion to a place at the Ministry of War. Given the conviction of Dreyfus's guilt by the army generals and the lack of any additional evidence (before 1898) besides the *petit-bleu* inculpating him, and aware of the widespread belief in a Jewish-led conspiracy to free a traitor and convict an innocent if unsavory officer, Esterhazy had reason to think he would be successful. Moreover, terrified by the threat to their own careers and reputations should the truth emerge, these generals did their best to shield Esterhazy from the charges raised against him. In letters to President Faure in October 1897, Esterhazy himself threatened that "diplomatic complications" with Germany would surface if his honor and name went unprotected. Then, on November 15, Mathieu openly denounced him as the traitor.

By this time, Esterhazy was no longer in active service. His reputation, if not his guilt, was a matter of public record. A spurned mistress, to whom he owed several thousand francs, had sent letters he had written years ago to the newspaper *Le Figaro*. The letters showed how much he despised France and the French military. "They were not worth the bullets to kill them."[10] Elsewhere he anticipated and looked forward to a German victory in another war. Facing bankruptcy, he was unable to sleep without resorting to opium. Then another devastating story broke. In the fall of 1896, he had taken money from a nephew, Christian Esterhazy, to invest, promising high rates of return thanks to alleged contacts with well-placed financiers. Instead, he had used the funds, among other ways, to buy a partnership in a house of prostitution. Even the minister of war, General Billot, when made aware of Esterhazy's scandalous behavior, preferred that he resign from the military. After having urged Drumont, Rochefort, and Cassagnac to launch a press campaign against his "incompetent" superiors, Esterhazy did so.

At his two-day trial in early January 1898, which he had demanded as his "right" to clear his name, Esterhazy eloquently played the part of an innocent soldier who had been unjustly slandered. In deliberations that lasted less than three minutes, he was acquitted by his military judges. It appeared that he could never be legally convicted of having written the *bordereau*, and the case against Dreyfus seemed closed. It was then that Zola published his famous letter.

In late April 1898, Christian Esterhazy, who had believed his uncle to be innocent, was insulted by him when he asked for an accounting of the funds entrusted to Esterhazy to invest. Christian now told Mathieu and Joseph Reinach that he was willing to testify regarding his uncle's complicity with the General Staff to make Picquart repudiate his findings. The net was closing about Esterhazy. In his July 7, 1898, speech, War Minister Cavaignac, although insistent on Dreyfus's guilt, made it clear that Esterhazy had dishonored his uniform and would face punishment.

News of Henry's forgery and subsequent suicide convinced Esterhazy of just how dangerous his situation had become. At first, he tried to dismiss the confession as meaningless, but after Henry's suicide, he fled to Belgium and then Britain. There he admitted to having written the *bordereau* but on the orders of Colonel Sandherr (who conveniently died in 1897 and could not contradict him) to feed the Germans false information. This defense was elaborated on in a slim volume that Esterhazy published at the end of the year, *Le Dessous de l'Affaire Dreyfus* (The Underside of the Dreyfus Affair), in which he attempted to portray himself as a martyr. But because he had admitted writing the *bordereau*, some anti-Dreyfusards concluded that the corrupt Esterhazy had been paid to confess by the Jewish-financed "syndicate," an interpretation accepted by diehards who continued to believe in Dreyfus's guilt. Because Esterhazy had previously denied authorship of the *bordereau* when first charged with doing so, however, a majority of the French now rejected anything he said.

Under a grant of immunity given in early 1899, Esterhazy came to Paris to give evidence to the High Court. He repeated his story of having acted on orders but was further discredited when an artillery captain and one-time friend of Esterhazy recalled the latter's efforts to train at an artillery camp (and so acquire salable information). The captain's testimony provided more ammunition for the Dreyfusard forces. Esterhazy subsequently refused to testify at the Rennes court-martial; he only sent a letter repeating the lies in his book.

Aside from self-imposed exile, Esterhazy never paid for his crimes. He found his first few years in England difficult: he had no money, he was embittered, and he said that the Jews had "destroyed" him and the army had "deserted" him. But the death of an uncle provided a small inheritance, and his talent to entrance women resurfaced, yielding money and consolation. He eventually got work (using false names) as a journalist and was able to purchase a comfortable house. The hostility to the French Army endured, and during World War I, his critical articles nearly had his editor in France "shot for subversion."

Depending on the source relied on, Esterhazy got rich either as a "traveling salesman" or as the "drug-addicted manager of a brothel"—and perhaps from hush money sent by former French officers desperate to salvage their reputations. In any case, Esterhazy prospered because of his "salesmanship." He lived out his remaining years in England and died in 1923.

Hubert Joseph Henry (1846–1898)

Henry, who served in the Statistical Service, testified at the first court-martial that Dreyfus was the traitor, and to seal Dreyfus's guilt he began forging incriminating documents. His later arrest and confession marked a turning point in the Affair.

Coming from a farming family in a village in the Marne Department, Henry received a rudimentary education. Gruff and bull chested, he lacked many of the social graces. However, he was a veteran of the 1870 War (a sergeant promoted to second lieutenant), possessed enormous energy and ambition, and revealed a willingness to follow all orders. An avid reader of *La Libre Parole*, he had no doubts about the "perils of Jewish infiltration." He was assigned to the Statistical Service in 1877, where he made a poor impression; was sent to Algeria and later to Indo-china; and was promoted to major in 1893. At General Boisdeffre's request, he was reassigned to Intelligence the following year.

Henry's testimony at Dreyfus's 1894 trial dominated the proceedings. He asked to be recalled as a witness—specifically to be questioned about the "presence of a traitor" in the Statistical Section of the General Staff. "In a loud voice" and with sweeping gestures, he wished to go on record that "an absolutely honorable person" had told him so and had later identified the officer in question. "There he is," Henry shouted, pointing to Dreyfus: "That man is the traitor."[11]

Dreyfus's lawyer protested Henry's testimony as hearsay and asked the name of the informant. Henry was aware of the judges' respect for the army's concern with confidentiality, and when they asked him "on his honor" whether it was indeed Dreyfus, he turned to the crucifix on the wall behind them and said, "I swear it." This exchange marked the basic issue in the Dreyfus Affair: Could the word of a prisoner, a Jewish prisoner, stand up to that of a General Staff officer, a veteran, a friend of the men who made up the tribunal, a soldier with access to the most sensitive documents and now under oath? The seven judges took Henry at his word.

During the next three years, Henry continued to insist that the General Staff possessed "proof of Dreyfus's treachery" but that national security permitted no disclosure. Implicitly encouraged by his superiors, Henry set about ensuring that the proof was adequate: he began to manufacture it. When he was given a draft telegram from Schwartzkoppen to Berlin stating that the German military attaché had no knowledge of Dreyfus, Henry doctored the wording to show that he did. When a note taken from the German embassy wastebasket containing the phrase, "for P. . . has brought me many interesting things," Henry changed the "P" to a "D." Most famous was his alteration of the casual message from the Italian military attaché to his German counterpart—the torn-up message that, again, thanks to Madame Bastian (the cleaning woman working for French Intelligence) was taken from the wastebasket and brought to Henry on November 1, 1896. Henry kept the original salutation and signature and on similar paper substituted his own message implicating Dreyfus, taping the authentic parts of the letter to it. This is what came to be known as the "false Henry" or the "Henry forgery." Finally, Henry hired a professional forger, and both men created letters supposedly from Dreyfus to the kaiser (the German emperor) and from the kaiser to the German ambassador in Paris naming Dreyfus as a spy working for them. As head of the Statistical Service, Henry worked to protect Esterhazy, at one point sending du Paty and another officer disguised in false beards and dark glasses to calm the anxious Esterhazy in a Paris park.

When confronted by Cavaignac on August 30, 1898, Henry admitted that he had "added Dreyfus's name to an insignificant diplomatic note" but had done so "to calm his worried superiors." He had acted "to save the honor of the Army" and "solely in the interests of my country." Nevertheless, he was arrested. Twenty-four hours later, in his cell in the Mont-

Valérian prison, he was found with his throat cut. Some close friends doubted his suicide. But Henry knew that he would do more harm to his beloved army if he remained alive. Anti-Dreyfusards made use of *La Libre Parole* to solicit contributions for his widow to cover her costs in the suit for libel that she brought against Joseph Reinach, who had claimed that Henry had been Esterhazy's accomplice in treason. The quarter of a million contributions, accompanied by anti-Semitic and anti-Dreyfusard messages, received amounted to over 130,000 francs. The messages referred to Henry as a "victim of duty" and as a "martyr."[12] He was seen by his sympathizers as "a patriot" who took his own life when his attempts to protect the army had failed.

Jean Jaurès (1859–1914)

Jaurès was the Socialist leader who, having become convinced of Dreyfus's innocence, persuaded his party and numerous others of the need to reopen the case.

He was born in the southern French city of Castres. His father was a farmer. A brilliant student, Jaurès attended the prestigious *Ecole Normale*, where he studied philosophy. He then taught at the *lycée* (secondary school) in Albi and in 1883 at the University of Toulouse. His doctoral thesis, "On the Actuality of the Sentient World," was published in 1891, but in the interim his interests had turned to politics. Jaurès was elected a deputy from the Tarn Department in 1885 but failed to win reelection four years later. He evolved from radicalism (in the France of the 1880s, a progressive liberalism) to socialism, as revealed by articles published in the newspapers *La Dépêche de Toulouse* and *La Petite République*. He had become increasingly disenchanted with conservative social policies, and a great miners' strike at Carmaux sealed his commitment to socialism, which he saw as the logical outcome of France's Third Republic. It was as a Socialist that he was returned to the Chamber of Deputies in 1893. With a short, stocky build—Jaurès called himself "a cultured peasant"—he proved a magnificent orator who dazzled his listeners, whether parliamentarians, workers, or academics. He never accepted an orthodox Marxist materialism but called for an idealistic, "integral" socialism committed to bringing social justice to France.

Like so many others at the time of Dreyfus's 1894 court-martial, Jaurès saw no reason to doubt the condemned captain's guilt and could only wonder whether the culprit's wealth had allowed him to avoid the death penalty. Would such mercy have been shown to a proletarian? The contradiction between the death penalty for a private striking an officer and the leniency shown to a traitor persuaded Jaurès to submit a bill abolishing the death penalty for the former offense. His speech was so in·emperate that the Chamber censured and temporarily barred him froi ι its sessions.

Even as the need to reopen the case became clear, many Socialists, showing little affection for an army used to quell strikes ("Dreyfus would have fired on us"), preferred to remain neutral in a conflict between a rich officer and the generals who had condemned him. "The proletariat," thundered the orthodox Marxist Jules Guesde, "has no right to bestow its pity."[13] It was also true that in identifying capitalism with a few wealthy Jews (the Rothschild name was symbolic here), an economically (rather than a racially) based anti-Semitism was embraced by many within Socialist ranks. With such Dreyfusard stalwarts as Joseph Reinach and Scheurer-Kestner vehemently opposed to socialism, it was understandable that Jaurès limited himself to pointing out the irregularities in the case. Why was there no investigation of these irregularities? he asked. As late as January 22, 1898, when the government's charges against Zola were debated in the Chamber, Jaurès took advantage of the narrowly focused accusation to score political points against the conservative Méline ministry. But when Prime Minister Méline in turn accused Socialists of calling for revolutionary violence in the Dreyfus Affair, an enraged Jaurès cried that it was the refusal to acknowledge the "non-disclosures, ambiguities, and acts of cowardice" that were responsible for any violence.[14]

It was the respected librarian of the *Ecole Normale*, Lucien Herr, who persuaded Jaurès and others, including the young Léon Blum, of Dreyfus's innocence and of the procedural irregularities that had led to his conviction. Jaurès's basic humanity overcame his class bias and led him to conclude that justice is the right of every individual, regardless of how well born.

As a witness for Zola, Jaurès demanded to know why at the Esterhazy trial the relevant documents were discussed behind closed doors; he supposed that the object was less "truth and justice" than a "vindication of the army chiefs." War Minister Mercier had not even shared these documents with his colleagues in the government. If such procedures were tolerated, Jaurès said, "it will be the end of any liberty or justice."

Jaurès now wanted to go further on Dreyfus's behalf, although Socialists in Parliament feared that support of Dreyfus would cost them votes in the 1898 general legislative elections. Their manifesto calling for neutrality did not address the question of the captain's guilt. When the elections, marked by a groundswell of nationalist feeling, cost several Socialists their seats, including Jaurès himself, their fears proved justified.

After Cavaignac's July 7 speech citing the documents used to convict Dreyfus, an ebullient Jaurès proclaimed that precisely because the minister quoted from what had to be forgeries, he had inadvertently guaranteed that the Affair was far from over. In an open letter published in the Socialist newspaper *La Petite République*, Jaurès criticized Cavaignac for using documents that formed the basis of Dreyfus's conviction when those documents had never been mentioned in the indictment. Jaurès specifically denounced the document produced by Henry to save Esterhazy as "the most crude and blatant forgery." Even so, other Socialist leaders refused to abandon their neutrality.

Now, with more time made available by his electoral defeat, Jaurès set out to provide the proof that forgeries had taken place. On August 10, 1898, he published the first in a series of articles—later collected in a pamphlet, *Les Preuves* (The Evidence). Having finally and definitively proclaimed Dreyfus innocent, the articles carefully traced all the irregularities and illegalities in the proceedings that led to Dreyfus's conviction and Esterhazy's acquittal. He told his Socialist colleagues that as a victim of injustice, Dreyfus was entitled to their support. As Zola had done with intellectuals, Jaurès brought Socialists to the Dreyfusard cause. In so doing, he consolidated left-wing support for the "bourgeois" republic and did much to break the hold of anti-Semitism on the far left. It was not coincidental that the first Jewish prime minister in France was a Socialist and the first Socialist prime minister was a Jew (Léon Blum) . Dreyfus was now seen as an innocent victim of injustice, a symbol of all who suffer and are oppressed, and not as a Jew or an army officer. For Jaurès, Socialists participated in the larger struggle for humanity by defending Dreyfus.

When Waldeck-Rousseau invited the new leader of the parliamentary Socialists (after Jaurès's electoral defeat), Alexandre Millerand, to sit in a government of republican defense and bring to it the support of the far left, Millerand was accused by Guesde of betraying the Socialist cause by participating in a non-Socialist government. He did so, orthodox Marxists charged, because of personal ambition. However, Jaurès defended Millerand and the principle of "ministerial participation" by a Socialist as furthering the cause of working-class reform as well as defending the Republic from the threat of clerico-military reaction. This split in Socialist ranks would prevent the various factions from forming a united party for several years to come.

On hearing of the new government's offer to pardon Dreyfus, Jaurès, like Clemenceau, wanted to continue the struggle for total vindication. The Affair loomed larger than the individual. A pardon, he believed, was equivalent to a defeat. But when persuaded that a third court-martial would only reconvict the ailing Dreyfus, he agreed that the Dreyfusard camp should accept the pardon provided that Dreyfus continue to seek justice and have his innocence declared.

Jaurès sought to reopen the case in 1903, for which he was condemned by the disenchanted Charles Péguy, who saw the Dreyfus cause degenerate into a political morass. Jaurès's speech to the Chamber of Deputies on April 16 retold the complicity of the generals, the ministers, the nationalist and anti-Semitic leagues, and elements of the clergy. To justify the renewed quest for revision, he specifically raised the matter of the "original" *bordereau* that the German emperor was supposed to have personally annotated. (At the risk of provoking war, General Mercier had threatened to disclose the original "annotated" *bordereau*—the one received at the Statistical Section was only an "onionskin tracing"—should Dreyfus's conviction have been overturned. Never found, the "annotated *bordereau*" had become part of anti-Dreyfusard legend.) As a consequence of Jaurès's speech, the deputies voted to have the Combes government investigate. Its minister of war, General André, did so and advised the high court to convene in order to reconsider the guilty verdict. Jaurès and others testified before it, and finally, on June 12, 1906, the court quashed the verdict and stipulated there would not be another.

Jaurès became the great opponent of Clemenceau's antilabor policies during the remainder of the decade, and the struggle between the two men defined French politics until the outbreak of World War I. He and his now unified Socialist party joined with Radicals in a *bloc des gauches* (left-wing coalition) in an anticlerical campaign that led to the separation of church and state in 1905. When the various Socialist factions formed a single party theoretically committed to revolutionary action and no cooperation with non-Socialists, Jaurès reluctantly agreed and played a leadership role. He became more radical in his last years, showing sympathy for revolutionary syndicalism, that is, for a more militant trade-unionism, but focused his efforts on staving off war. It was at the height of this campaign that he was assassinated by a nationalist fanatic on July 31, 1914.

Auguste Mercier (1833–1921)

General Mercier was the minister of war who ordered the Dreyfus court-martial in 1894. Although attacked at the time the case was re-opened, he never denied the charge of treason raised against Dreyfus.

Mercier was born in Arras (northern France) and trained at the elite engineering school, the *Polytechnique*. He began his military career by serving in Mexico and fought in the Franco-Prussian War. Having developed political ambitions, Mercier was named minister of war in the 1893–1894 cabinet of Jean Casimir-Périer. A tall, slim—or gaunt (depending on one's perspective)—sixty year old, he wore a gray mustache, and his eyes seemed perpetually half-closed. Described as "puritanical," "authoritarian," and "abrupt," he was concerned with advancing his career.

When the *bordereau* first came to his attention on September 28, 1894, Mercier appeared "frantic" and reacted hastily. Such behavior contrasted with that customarily shown: he was commonly considered "cold," "methodical," and "resolute," possessed of patience and devoid of emotion. His commitment to the Republic (many officers favored a royalist restoration) and a reputation for "level-headedness" had accounted for his nomination as war minister. His first months in the office suggested he had been a brilliant choice. When the previous December an anarchist hurled a bomb into the Chamber, frightened deputies were seen crawling under their desks. The seated war minister calmly removed a splinter and casually asked his neighbor, "Does this belong to you?" Six months later, Mercier was retained in his post by the new prime minister, Charles Dupuy, and was seen as a star of his government.

Then his star began to fall. When he rejected an inventor's "self-propelled" bullet, he inadvertently told the Chamber he did so because of his "gunner's flair," by which he meant his artilleryman's intuition. The choice of words was derided by his critics. In the summer of 1894, he prematurely demobilized 60,000 army conscripts, creating a manpower shortage, and he had to rescind the order. Newspapers stepped up their criticism. Mercier was questioned in Parliament, and rumors flew of his imminent dismissal.

These mishaps threatened to end any dreams he had of higher political office. Mercier needed a triumph, not an unresolved espionage case that might prove disastrous. Such was his frame of mind when news of the purloined *bordereau* reached him. Although his first impression was that Dreyfus' was guilty—and Mercier usually relied on first impressions—he ordered his staff to "get to the bottom" of the treason that would "ruin him or save him." The traitor had to be a trainee on the General Staff. Dreyfus fitted the profile sketched, and when the first handwriting expert called, from the Bank of France, doubted that Dreyfus was the author, Mercier had the self-styled expert who headed the Paris Police Department's Division of Criminal Records brought in. Bertillon was more positive. When the minister heard of the investigating officer's (du Paty's) tentative assessment of Dreyfus's guilt, he accepted it as conclusive.

He believed he had to. Fearful that Dupuy was looking for an excuse to fire him and that accusations of delay in identifying the culprit would give Dupuy the pretext to do so, Mercier was convinced that the traitor had to be found at once. He also feared being accused of showing favoritism to Jews. Shortly before the arrival of the *bordereau*, he had quashed the conviction of a Jewish army doctor without awaiting the decision of a military tribunal. The anti-Semitic press in general, and Drumont's newspaper in particular, would find him a champion of Judaism. Accordingly, Mercier told his subordinates he wanted Dreyfus arrested and "definitive proof" of his guilt found. When disagreement among the handwriting experts momentarily led du Paty to urge that the arrest order be cancelled, Mercier disingenuously informed him that both the president and prime minister had approved it.

The search for evidence was entrusted to the head of the Statistical Section, Colonel Jean-Conrad Sandherr, an impassioned anti-Semite. One important discovery was an earlier note recovered by Madame Bastian from Schwartzkoppen's office, from the German military attaché to his Italian counterpart (Germany and Italy were then allied), Colonel Alessandro Panizzardi, referring to "this scoundrel D" (*ce canaille de D*). Actually, the note implicated a civilian clerk named Dubois, who had been discovered a year earlier. Because the note might prove useful, it was added to the file of documents and sent to General Boisdeffre, the chief of staff, and to Mercier.

The war minister knew that he had no solid evidence and that Dreyfus had not confessed. His political future became even more precarious when *La Libre Parole* identified Dreyfus as the officer arrested in its issue of November 1 and reported that Mercier had received Jewish threats to delay action. The charge sealed the campaign waged by the nationalist and anti-Semitic press against Mercier for permitting the "breakdown of military order" and for failing to rid the General Staff of "treasonous Jews, Protestants, and Freemasons." Consequently, the minister reassured skeptical cabinet members that his evidence was "watertight," and they approved the order to begin legal proceedings. In an interview with a reporter from *Le Figaro* on November 28, Mercier claimed that Dreyfus's guilt was "absolute" and "certain." Dupuy ordered him to retract his remarks (no trial, after all, had yet taken place), but the damage was done.

It was by no means clear that an open trial would convict Dreyfus. Even President Faure, no supporter of the victim, believed that the accused captain would be acquitted. Aware of the limited and wholly circumstantial evidence and fearful his career was at an end—years later he admitted he "would have preferred to have taken more time, but newspaper disclosures had made it impossible,"[15]—Mercier pressed at once for a closed trial. In a clear violation of Dreyfus's rights, the war minister secretly sent the "scoundrel D" letter and other material to the judges.

It was true that Drumont, Rochefort, and others in the nationalist press complained throughout November that no action had been taken. Dreyfus, they pointed out, had been arrested on October 15, yet no trial date was set. Why the delay? With the decision to go ahead, and particularly after the guilty verdict was rendered, the "attacks" against Mercier came to a abrupt end, and he was hailed as a hero by those who had repeatedly denounced him as "negligent" and "stupid." Congratulations poured in, and the minister's earlier sins were forgiven. His approval rating soared when legislation he inspired was enacted in the Chamber of Deputies on February 9. It reinstated Devil's and neighboring islands off the South American coast as official "places of deportation." They had been used as penal colonies by both Napoleons, but Third Republic politicians had preferred the less enervating climate of New Caledonia in the South Pacific.

After the military tribunal sentenced the prisoner and aware that he had illegally sent incriminating documents to the court, Mercier ordered Sandherr to remove the evidence and replace the respective pieces in their original folders. Whether out of negligence or a commitment to routine, Sandherr failed to obey; the Dreyfus file was locked up, and so preserved. When Dreyfus's sister, writing on behalf of the family, appealed to the war minister's "honesty" and "patriotism" and asked him to overturn the decision of a secret court that had refused to reveal the evidence relied on to secure a conviction, Mercier did not bother to reply.

In 1895, the president of the Republic, Jean Casimir-Périer, resigned after only a few months in office. He had complained about not being kept adequately informed on a variety of matters and had tired of the incessant attacks against him in the Chamber of Deputies. Mercier let his name be placed in nomination as Casimir-Périer's successor, on the grounds that he had brought a traitor before a court-martial. He secured only three votes from the assembled legislators. (The president was then elected by a joint session of the Chamber of Deputies and the Senate.) The suave Havre merchant-turned-politician, Félix Faure, was named. The new prime minister, Alexandre Ribot, replaced Mercier at the Ministry of War with another general, Emile Zurlinden, who took his predecessor's advice about sending Dreyfus to Devil's Island. Mercier was reassigned to command an army corps northwest of Paris.

In his famous letter, Zola accused Mercier of "having made himself an accomplice in one of the greatest crimes in history, probably because of a weak mind." With other army officers, Mercier contributed to Drumont's subscription drive on behalf of Madame Henry. It was his illegal use of the secret dossier, along with Henry's confession, that persuaded the High Court to order another trial. The charges against Mercier, however, were deferred, to await the outcome of the second court-martial. The trial portended a Mercier-versus-Dreyfus conflict, and on August 3, 1899, Mercier was quoted as predicting that Dreyfus would once again be convicted. "The guilty party," he said, "is either him or me."[16]

Mercier testified at Rennes along with other generals and war ministers. Although called only as a witness, he asked that a mistranslated Panizzardi telegram be added to the evidence and was not reprimanded by the judges for this irregularity. He let it be known to Dreyfus's lawyer Labori that he possessed a letter from Esterhazy compromising Labori's daughter, but this recourse to blackmail by a frightened general was shrugged off. The testimony of Mercier, once a sincere republican, showed how he had become a prisoner of his royalist supporters. He recited the now familiar litany, document after document, that comprised the prosecution's case, and then he dropped a bombshell: The kaiser himself was involved in espionage and may have communicated with Dreyfus. He had even annotated the original *bordereau* (the one retrieved by Madame Bastian had been a tracing). If revealed, the kaiser's involvement threatened war. The resulting uproar in the courtroom was such that a recess had to be called.

When the court reconvened, former President Casimir-Périer and Foreign Secretary Gabriel Hanotaux absolutely refuted Mercier's allegation about the threat of war, but the unruffled general only conceded an error in the date and stuck to his story. He then invented new evidence: Dreyfus had sold the Germans information about a new artillery shell and had provided a secret formula for an explosive. From the judges' perspective, no lawyer's refutations could stand up to the charges of military experts.

During the trial, it seemed that Mercier had included himself in the team of prosecutors. His introduction of evidence has already been noted. He spoke without the court's permission, sat at the judges' table, and cross-examined without interference. Labori, returned to the courtroom after an eight-day recovery from an attempted assassination, discredited Mercier's testimony: the general offered no proof that Germany had threatened war or that the kaiser had been involved, and he had sent trial documents to the judges. But Mercier proved a master of evasion and had recourse to ambiguity. To the last charge, for example, he countered that he had done so not as a general or minister but as an ordinary citizen doing his duty. If the general was diminished by his testimony, he survived. Again, because he would be guilty if Dreyfus were declared innocent, the military judges at Rennes chose the word of an active army general and not that of a once-convicted Jew.

In the Senate elections held in June 1900, the left won eighty of ninety-nine contested seats. Mercier, recently retired from the army, was one of the nine nationalists elected. Waldeck-Rousseau's amnesty bill was furiously denounced by Dreyfusards, who realized it denied Picquart and Zola any right to be exonerated and nullified all charges against Esterhazy—and Mercier. Inspired by Mathieu's belief that the "annotated *bordereau*" had been used by Mercier to influence the judges at Rennes, Jaurès's speech in April 1903 won the Chamber's approval to reopen the case. Testifying before the High Court, Mercier continued to insist on

Dreyfus's guilt, but the united court annulled the Rennes verdict and unanimously found Dreyfus innocent of all charges. Twenty-four hours later, the Chamber debated a vote of 473 to 2—passed a law reintegrating Dreyfus and Picquart into the army. When the measure reached the Senate, Mercier objected that the High Court had reached its decision behind closed doors. He apparently saw no irony in his remarks. He was shouted down: one senator cried that if not for the amnesty, Mercier would occupy Dreyfus's empty cell.

Mercier lived through World War I as "a pariah to the Left and as the petted relic of the Right." Three years after the war ended, he died, "a man,"described by Dreyfus in his memoirs as "devoid of moral sense."

Georges Picquart (1854–1914)

Picquart's discovery of the *petit-bleu* convinced him that the traitor was not Dreyfus but the dissolute and reprehensible Esterhazy.

Picquart, like Dreyfus, born in Alsace, came from an old and distinguished family of judges and career soldiers. He compiled a brilliant record at Saint-Cyr, France's military academy, and served in Algeria and Indochina in the 1880s. As a lieutenant at the *Ecole Supérieure de Guerre* (War College) between 1890 and 1893, he was one of Dreyfus's instructors, probably the only one left relatively unimpressed by him. Picquart acknowledged his student's energy and discipline, but criticized his "lack of imagination" and "unjustified self-confidence" and gave him low grades on map reading and field maneuvers. In June 1895, Picquart was assigned to head the Statistical Section. Fluent in German and able to read three other foreign languages (rare for a French officer), possessed of a "formidable" knowledge of military science, the youngest major in the army— he was promoted to lieutenant-colonel in early April 1896—Picquart could look forward to a bright future.

Like many other officers, he was also a convinced anti-Semite, but his intelligence and urbanity prevented overt displays of bigotry; rather, it took the form of polite indifference to Jews. Later, when Picquart acknowledged the prevalence of anti-Semitism in the General Staff, he admitted that at the time of Dreyfus's admission, "by assigning a Jewish trainee to a department not concerned with secret matters I would spare him certain embarrassments."[17] Also like his colleagues, Picquart initially accepted the guilty verdict. Still, when he attended the court-martial and learned how limited and circumstantial the evidence was, he believed an acquittal was likely. When he asked du Paty what could possibly have motivated the treason of a wealthy officer, the latter spoke of a large payment made to the Dreyfus family in the form of insurance coverage for a burned factory, an explanation mentioned only in passing at the trial. The real—and unspoken—reason was found in the context of anti-Semitism and specifically in the widespread assumption of anti-Semites that Jews had no country. When secret documents were supplied to the judges, Picquart had no reason to question their authenticity. At the degradation ceremony, noting Dreyfus's glance at the piled-up braid and buttons, Picquart was overheard to say that the traitor was estimating their value, "like a Jewish tailor."[18]

After Colonel Sandherr's death, Picquart became head of intelligence. Forty-one years old and now the youngest lieutenant-colonel in the French army, Picquart accepted his new assignment but did not relish the prospect of "sordid spying." He was told by Chief of Staff Boisdeffre that because the Jews would "mount an offensive" to free Dreyfus, he should "feed" the record with whatever additional information he found regarding motive.

Picquart came across the *petit-bleu* early in 1896. The unsent express delivery letter from Schwartzkoppen to Esterhazy had reached the Statistical Section by the usual route: Madam Bastian's wastebasket. Having seen Esterhazy's application to join the General Staff, he noted the similarity of its handwriting to that of the *bordereau*. Fearing another Dreyfus case, Picquart launched an investigation of Esterhazy. He learned how disreputable he was: his debts, his mistresses, his unfitness as an officer. He knew of his superiors' hostility to reopening the Dreyfus case and what his findings might mean for his career. Overcoming his own prejudices against the Jewish officer, he read the secret dossier, never destroyed, compiled against Dreyfus and came to the realization that the convict on Devil's Island was innocent.

It took moral courage and intellectual honesty to tell the generals what he had learned. He viewed their coolness ("What difference does it make if that Jew stays on Devil's Island?"), especially that of Deputy Chief of Staff General Charles Gonse, as incomprehensible. Picquart agreed that it would "open a Pandora's box," but did not the generals, and by now the minister of war, who had been alerted, realize that it was in the army's best interest to reveal the "error" rather than be accused of duplicity? When ordered to remain silent, Picquart told Gonse, "I will not carry this secret to my grave."[19]

To get him away from Paris, his superiors sent Picquart on inspection tours throughout the country and ultimately to North Africa. Aware of their wish to silence him and determined that the secret would not die with him (and after a riding accident alerted him to the fact that he had done nothing to ensure this), Picquart prepared a statement to be given to the president of the Republic in the event of his death. He also shared his discovery with his friend and lawyer Louis Leblois, after swearing him to secrecy.

Aware that it was the only way to help Picquart and Dreyfus, Leblois broke his vow to keep still and informed a vice president of the Senate, Auguste Scheurer-Kestner, who had shown an interest in the case. It was Picquart's "meddling" that prompted Colonel Henry, no friend of his, to resort to forgeries and alterations to demonstrate both Dreyfus's guilt and Picquart's "mistakes." When Henry lectured him on the need to show loyalty, Picquart had realized he was suspect and to protect himself had to help save Dreyfus. Informed by Esterhazy's banker that his client's handwriting matched that of the *bordereau* (placarded throughout Paris by Mathieu), Mathieu told Scheurer-Kestner. The senator then confirmed Esterhazy's culpability by divulging what Leblois had told him. Both the Dreyfus family and Picquart, by separate paths, had reached the same conclusion.

To implicate Picquart fully, Henry manufactured a letter tying him to the Jewish "syndicate." He then arranged for Esterhazy to address telegrams to Picquart alleging that the latter had fabricated the *petit-bleu*. He brought these telegrams to the minister of war in the newly formed Méline government, Jean-Baptiste Billot, and said they had been intercepted. Henry also retouched the *petit-bleu* by obliterating part of Esterhazy's name, then recopying it to suggest Picquart had committed a forgery. Unfortunately, Henry forgot that a photograph had been taken of the original.

The Esterhazy court-martial quickly turned into a trial against Picquart, who had named him as the traitor. Picquart's testimony was given behind closed doors, which publicly silenced him, and was contemptuously dismissed by the judges. Then, on January 12,1898, Picquart was arrested for passing secrets to Leblois, and a board of inquiry officially ordered his dismissal from the army. The generals did this because they anticipated what Picquart would say at the forthcoming Zola trial and wished to discredit him. However, War Minister Billot delayed implementation of the dismissal in order to keep Picquart under military discipline. When at the Zola trial, Henry accused Picquart of lying, the latter informed the court—and caused consternation—that Colonel Sandherr had told the Statistical Section to find additional evidence to complete the case against Dreyfus. Three days after Zola's conviction of February 26, 1898, Picquart was dismissed from the army.

In the months that followed, the generals resorted to character assassination of Picquart. On April 25, Gonse prepared a report to the effect that Picquart was homosexual and based this charge on an unidentified police report. This, he said, would explain Picquart's behavior in the Dreyfus case. Then, oblivious to the implicit contradiction, the deputy chief of staff informed a husband of his wife's infidelity with Picquart, hoping either for a duel with, or a lawsuit against, Picquart by the aggrieved husband. The only result was the breakup of a marriage.

On July 7, the newest and latest war minister, Godefroy Cavaignac, read "proofs" of Dreyfus's guilt, including the Henry forgery, to the Chamber of Deputies. The next day, Jaurès and Picquart challenged the authenticity of these "proofs." Picquart was arrested on charges of forgery on July 13. Aware of the forthcoming arrest, he publicly stated that if found dead in his cell, it would be murder and not suicide.

As with the prosecution of Dreyfus, Picquart was held in solitary confinement, was not told the exact charges, and was not allowed to see his lawyers. During his eleven-month internment, he became the most prominent symbol of the Dreyfusard cause. Demonstrations took place in the streets and in parliament. His supporters claimed that now that he was a civilian, he was no longer subject to military law, and anti-Dreyfusards were outraged when the Criminal Chamber of the High Court on December 8 indefinitely postponed the Picquart court-martial four days before it was to begin. It did so on the grounds that criminal proceedings must first take place (which was unlikely given the lack of credible evidence). Saved from military justice, Picquart remained in prison, although after March 3, 1899, when his case was transferred to a civil court, a civilian prison.

Not until June 2, 1899, after 300 days of confinement, was Picquart released. A civil court dismissed charges that he had fabricated the *petit-bleu*. He received a hero's welcome, and congratulatory telegrams poured in from around the world. As the Rennes court-martial of Dreyfus was to show, however, the Affair was not yet over. Picquart testified for seven hours; for one observer, "a masterpiece of reasoning, the intellectual triumph of the trial."[20] Picquart agreed with Clemenceau that Demange's strategy of raising reasonable doubt was useless in this military tribunal; he preferred Labori's more impassioned and frontal assault on the army. Picquart also opposed acceptance of the pardon offered to Dreyfus by Waldeck-Rousseau: he believed that Joseph Reinach—"a close associate of Waldeck"—had persuaded the Dreyfus family to accept in order "to buy political peace." Picquart was especially embittered by the amnesty law. He had been forced out of the army, but Mercier was free to run for the Senate.

During the course of the Affair, Picquart fought several duels—with Henry on March 5, 1898 (wounding Henry in the arm), and with Gonse (who missed and Picquart refused to fire), to name but two—but had refused Esterhazy's challenge in May 1898, preferring to do battle in the courtroom. On July 13, 1906, Picquart was reinstated into the army and promoted to the rank of brigadier general. When Clemenceau formed a government that year, he called on Picquart to serve as his minister of war. It was in this capacity that Picquart had to pass judgment on Dreyfus's application for promotion to lieutenant-colonel. (Unlike Picquart, he was not credited with the time spent while interned.) Still embittered by the latter's acceptance of a pardon, Picquart rejected the application, and Dreyfus thereupon asked to be retired from active service. (Earlier, at the time the High Court annulled the Rennes decision, Picquart had refused to shake the hand offered by Mathieu; he was sufficiently moved, however, to shake the hand extended by Dreyfus at the latter's reinstatement ceremony.)

In January 1914, Picquart was again thrown from a horse. He waved off medical treatment and died at his desk the following day.

Joseph Reinach (1856–1921)

One of the first Dreyfusards, Reinach was perhaps the most important active politician to side with the victim throughout the course of the Affair. He would write the seven-volume history of the Dreyfus Affair on which all historians rely.

Reinach was born in Paris, the son of a former bank clerk whose investments in the first French railroad companies enabled him to leave sizable legacies to Joseph and his two brothers. While the brothers became classical scholars, Reinach studied law. He wrote for Léon Gambetta's newspaper, *La République Française*, and in 1881 managed Gambetta's short-lived cabinet. Reinach became—and remained—an ardent defender of the new Third Republic. He served as secretary-general of the *Ligue des Patriotes* (League of Patriots) in the 1880s and after Gambetta's death succeeded him as director of the newspaper—and later wrote his biography.

Reinach was elected a deputy in 1889, defeating a Boulangist candidate in the Basses-Alpes Department, and was reelected in 1893. In the Chamber he made his patriotism—and opposition to socialism—clear and soon achieved a reputation as "the most prominent Jew in the French Parliament." Opponents repeatedly attacked his lineage: he was the nephew and son-in-law of Baron Jacques de Reinach, who had been implicated in the Panama scandal. Short and stocky, with a thick brown beard, Reinach behaved as pugnaciously as he looked. By the end of his career, he would have fought thirteen duels. His appearance, however, belied his interest in the arts: he collected paintings and would leave many to the Louvre.

At the time of Dreyfus's arrest, Reinach questioned his guilt and lobbied for an open trial. After the verdict was handed down, he worked tirelessly to raise doubts among the cultural and political elite and succeeded in arousing the skepticism in the case shown by Senator Scheurer-Kestner. By 1897, both men were working to have the case reopened. Reinach's articles in the newspaper *Le Siècle* triggered the diatribes of the nationalist press, particularly after Esterhazy was accused of writing the *bordereau*. Together with other Dreyfusards, Reinach was accused of belonging to a Jewish "syndicate" that sought to betray France. Days before the Esterhazy trial opened, Reinach and Mathieu Dreyfus arranged for publication of the 1894 indictment, proving that the *bordereau* was the only evidence admitted into the court. Reinach's request that Dreyfus's conviction therefore be annulled—on the grounds that documents given to the judges were never shown to the defense—was ignored.

Drumont's reply to Zola's *"J'accuse"* letter came as an open letter of his own to President Faure accusing Reinach of having slandered Esterhazy. After Cavaignac's July 7 (1898) speech stating he had "irrefutable proof" of Dreyfus's treason, Reinach and the Dreyfusard lawyers decided that Picquart should denounce the secret documents relied on by the authorities as forgeries.

As a thoroughly assimilated Jew—indeed, a free-thinker—Reinach, unlike Bernard-Lazare, never saw his support of Dreyfus in religious terms. So closely did he identify himself with the French Republic that his Dreyfusism was seen as a manifestation of patriotism. He rejected any idea of Jewish nationalism as antithetical to love of country. Zionism, and specifically the first Zionist Congress, held in 1897, put some sort of ethnic solidarity over the national interest. For Reinach, Zionism was "an anachronism in modern society," and the prospect that it might take precedence over support for France horrified him. Later historians have criticized him for exaggerating the role of the Jesuit order in promoting nationalist anti-Semitism. Still, the attempts of other Catholic orders, particularly the Assumptionist Fathers and their anti-Semitic and anti-Republican newspaper, *La Croix*, as well as the silence from the Vatican, had lent credence to his charges of church complicity.

As one of the few candidates to refer to the Affair in the 1898 legislative elections, Reinach was defeated. Because he had accused her husband of being Esterhazy's accomplice (no hard evidence emerged to support this charge), Madame Henry sued Reinach for libel and was supported by Drumont and the anti-Dreyfusards. After the Rennes court-martial found Dreyfus once again guilty, Reinach suggested a pardon when told that a return to prison would kill the captain within six months. Moreover, a pardon offered immediately after the verdict would stand as a direct repudiation of it. Reinach told Mathieu that a pardon would dissociate France from "the cry of horror" that would resonate throughout the world when it learned of the court's decision. He also admitted it would bring to an end the "heroic phase" of the Affair, as Clemenceau and Jaurès recognized. Aware that Reinach was a friend of Waldeck, and believing that a pardon—and later the ministry's acceptance of the amnesty voted by the legislature—purchased political peace for the government, Picquart never forgave Reinach or the Dreyfus brothers for accepting both.

Reinach was reelected by his constituency in 1906 but lost his seat in 1914. In 1911, he completed the final volume of the massive history of the Affair that he had begun ten years before. In 1912, his only son, Adolphe (whose death in World War I would leave Reinach devastated), married Mathieu Dreyfus's daughter Marguerite. Reinach became *Le Figaro*'s military commentator during the war and the peace conference that followed, before his death in 1921.

Auguste Scheurer-Kestner (1833–1899)

Scheurer-Kestner was one of the few legislators to call for reopening the Dreyfus case through open letters to public officials, parliamentary speeches, and newspaper articles. Scheurer-Kestner was an Alsatian, like Dreyfus and Picquart, but from a great Protestant family of industrialists. Trained in science, he turned to politics, and because of his efforts to promote the republican cause under the Second Empire he was imprisoned by Louis Napoleon Bonaparte's government. As a deputy from Alsace, he was one of the last to serve in that capacity before the German annexation of the province, and as an important ally of Gambetta, he fervently defended the new Third Republic. Indeed, seen as one of the founding fathers of the Republic, he was elected one of the senators for life in 1875. With a tall, angular frame and long white beard, he looked the part of a distinguished elder statesman, and in 1896 he became a vice president of the Senate.

Like so many others, Scheurer-Kestner accepted the unanimously rendered guilty verdict, although the arrest of Dreyfus had troubled him. He wondered what could have motivated the wealthy officer, whose Alsatian backgound was well thought of, to commit an act of treason. After hearing the doubts of Joseph Reinach and Arthur Ranc, Scheurer-Kestner sought additional information but was left dissatisfied by official explanations.

Consequently, he willingly received Mathieu Dreyfus, who appealed on behalf of the family to another Alsatian. The senator expressed "great pity," according to his own account, but offered no direct support. At a dinner party, an officer involved in the preliminary investigation voiced confidence in the verdict on the grounds that Dreyfus had bought an expensive Paris home with German money. When he learned the alleged purchase was based on unfounded rumor, Scheurer-Kestner's confidence in the investigation was shaken. An unjustly condemned innocent man was an affront to the Republic, he thought.

When on July 13 1897, Picquart's lawyer, Leblois, swearing the senator to secrecy, told him of Picquart's belief in Esterhazy's guilt, Scheurer-Kestner was "staggered." And when shown Deputy Chief of Staff Gonse's letters to Picquart urging prudence, he was "absolutely floored." The next day Scheurer-Kestner told his fellow senators that he was convinced of Dreyfus's innocence. Because he was bound by oath not to provide details, however, he was listened to in polite silence.

He told others, including Lucie Dreyfus, that he had proof and that when Parliament reconvened, he would try to get the case reopened. Unable to divulge Esterhazy's name, he tried to provide leads for Mathieu—for example, that the real traitor came from an aristocratic backgound and had a hyphenated last name. However, too many French army officers fit that description for the clue to prove useful. Scheurer-Kestner hoped that Picquart himself, "an honest man," would speak out. "His honesty must not stop midway."[21] His inability to reveal Picquart's evidence left him vulnerable to the nationalist and anti-Semitic press. He was derided as a "naive old man" and a key player in a "Jew-loving Huguenot cabal." For "real Frenchmen," Alsatians were "the equivalent of Prussians." Some supporters of Scheurer-Kestner compared him to Voltaire, but the senator was not about to embarrass his beloved Republic and warned that the victim's religion should not be emphasized.

On October 29, Scheurer-Kestner visited President Faure, whom he had helped elect, in the Elysée Palace (the president's official residence). He left disappointed. Not without some justification, Faure reminded him he had only an uncorroborated story told by an officer who refused to make his accusations public. In any case, the matter was in the hands of the minister of war, General Billot, who would not open an inquiry.

When on November 6 or 7, Mathieu finally learned the name of the traitor (again, from Esterhazy's former banker who had noticed that the handwriting of the published *bordereau* matched that of his one-time client), he rushed to tell Scheurer-Kestner, who, obviously relieved, confirmed it.

To pave the way for his request to have the case reopened, Scheurer-Kestner sent an open letter to the newspaper *Le Temps* on November 14 arguing that "new facts" had surfaced that "prove the innocence of the condemned man" and that "a judicial error" had been made. He also related his unsuccessful efforts to have War Minister Billot reopen the investigation. A sympathetic deputy then tried to frighten Esterhazy by declaring in *Le Figaro* that not Dreyfus but another officer had written the *bordereau*. With no name divulged, the threat proved too vague. When another officer, not Esterhazy, was suspected, Mathieu was pressured on November 15 to identify Esterhazy as the author.

Two days earlier, on November 13, Scheurer-Kestner had sought to enlist the support of Emile Zola. He brought Leblois and the writer Marcel Prévost to meet the great novelist, and after obtaining additional details from Bernard-Lazare, Zola agreed to join the Dreyfusard camp. Together with Ranc, Scheurer-Kestner also convinced Georges Clemenceau that at the very least, gross irregularities had marred the Dreyfus trial. The alarmed Esterhazy planned to sue Mathieu and Scheurer-Kestner but was persuaded by his lawyer instead to ask for a military court-martial. On December 7, 1897, in a long-awaited speech to the Senate, Scheurer-Kestner rejected the charges against him brought by the nationalist press. But because he was forbidden to cite Gonse's letters to Picquart warning him to keep silent, his recitation of events contained no revelations. On the other hand, his efforts intensified the campaign of vilification by the anti-Dreyfusard press. He was a prominent member of the Jewish "syndicate" and was in the pay of Germany. Students demonstrated in front of his house. But foreign sentiment was strongly favorable, and in his memoirs Scheurer-Kestner told of the messages of support. It was to the senator that a former mistress of Esterhazy, owed money by him, brought letters written earlier by Esterhazy belittling the French and the army. The letters were published in the November 28, 1897, issue of *Le Figaro*.

When Zola considered writing his famous letter of accusation, Scheurer-Kestner worried about the wisdom of placing the writer at the mercy of a jury. At his trial, Zola included the senator among his witnesses, and the court heard Scheurer-Kestner question General Billot's good faith. However, when he tried to read Gonse's letter to Picquart, he was denied permission to do so by the judges. Afterward, ill from the cancer that was to kill him, weary, and disgusted by all the turmoil, Scheurer-Kestner no longer played an active role in the Dreyfus Affair.

Republicans tried to avoid mentioning the Affair in the 1898 legislative elections, fearing retribution at the hands of nationalist voters. Their fears proved well founded. Together with the defeats of such Dreyfusard deputies as Reinach and Jaurès, Scheurer-Kestner failed to win reelection as vice president of the Senate. He died on September 19, 1899, the same day that Dreyfus was pardoned. When in 1906 Dreyfus was reinstated into the army and Zola's ashes were transferred to the Panthéon, the Senate voted to place a bust of Scheurer-Kestner in its gallery of honor.

René Waldeck-Rousseau (1846–1904)

The conservative senator, who put together a national unity government to bring an end to the Affair. Waldeck-Rousseau was born in Nantes (Brittany), where he studied and practiced law. He was elected a deputy

in 1879 and joined Gambetta's short-lived ministry of November 1881-
January 1882. For promoting legislation in 1884 that recognized the
legality of trade unions, he acquired a reputation as an "enlightened conservative." He continued to practice law, becoming one of the country's
most prominent attorneys. Waldeck defended Gustave Eiffel in the Panama
case in 1893. The next year he was elected a senator and then ran, un-
successfully, in the presidential election of 1895, defeated by the Havre
merchant Félix Faure.

On learning of his brother's arrest, Mathieu Dreyfus first asked
Waldeck to act as Alfred's counsel. Waldeck refused, pleading unfamiliar-
ity with military courts and no doubt fearing the political repercussions
of taking an unpopular defense. He recommended Demange, who accepted. When War Minister Mercier let it be known to the press before
the first court-martial that he was convinced of Dreyfus's guilt, Waldeck,
at Demange's request, protested to the prime minister. But another request
by Demange—that he appeal to the president of the Republic to have an
open trial—was refused on constitutional grounds.

In 1897, as a Progressist (moderate republican) senator, Waldeck
favored a review of the case. Two years later, in late February 1899, he
protested the transfer of the review from the Criminal Chamber of the High
Court (the Chamber attacked by anti-Dreyfusards for its liberal leanings
and its Jewish president) to the court sitting as a whole. His protest won
favor in the Dreyfusard camp.

On June 4, 1899, President Loubet, suspected by anti-Dreyfusards
of cooperating with the victim's supporters, was assaulted (caned) by a
young aristocrat at the Auteuil racetrack. A vote taken a few days later
stressing the need to defend republican institutions signaled the end of
the Dupuy ministry. The fifty-two-year-old Waldeck-Rousseau, a centrist
Republican with authority and prestige, was named to form a new
government. Cold and aloof (the young Progressist lawyer and deputy
Raymond Poincaré, confronting him in a courtroom, described the experience as equivalent to a "poodle barking at a statue"), Waldeck put together
a cabinet of "republican defense." To control the army, he chose General
Gaston Galliffet as his minister of war, the man who had led a cavalry
charge at Sedan and had mercilessly executed remaining communards in
1871. To secure support from the left, he selected as his minister of commerce Alexandre Millerand, the leader of the parliamentary Socialists. At
first neutral in the Affair, Millerand switched to the Drefusard cause after

Henry's confession. He had made a reputation for himself defending Socialists and labor leaders in court and promoted a "reformist"strategy—one that abjured violence and accepted "gradualist" or legislative means to secure Socialist ends—and consequently urged his fellow Socialists to accept France's Third Republic.

Left-wing deputies fiercely objected to Galliffet and those on the right to Millerand. Both sides called the newly named government "one of all contradictions," and only after a stormy session did Waldeck narrowly win a vote of confidence. With Parliament recessed for the summer, the government enjoyed three months of freedom to take action. Reinach, who approved, acknowledged it was a virtual dictatorship. Waldeck had Paul Déroulède, who had attempted a coup, arrested. Galliffet dismissed or relocated the top generals. Such steps seemed necessary in view of a perceived nationalist uprising. Protest meetings calling for sedition were sweeping the country, a general on the Superior War Council threatened "action" if "calumnies" against the army continued, and rumors of troop movements were heard. The League of Patriots joined with supporters of the duke of Orléans to bring down the republican regime. The leader of the Anti-Semitic League, Jules Guérin, conspired to assassinate Dreyfus's lawyer, Labori, at the Rennes trial but succeeded only in wounding him. Guérin and some followers barricaded themselves in a house on the rue Chabrol, and fearing to take stronger action, the government ordered police to lay siege to the house. Fed by sympathizers who hurled provisions from the upper deck of passing buses, the "siege of Fort Chabrol" took on the dimensions of a farce until a surrender was achieved. Waldeck's appeal to Germany to allow Schwartzkoppen to testify or, at the least, hand over some of the documents listed in the *bordereau*, went unheeded. Berlin had already denied any ties to Dreyfus and preferred to see discord continue. Convinced of the impossibility of a legal solution and that a third court-martial would convict Dreyfus again, Waldeck, at the family's request, offered to pardon Dreyfus. Later, on January 1, 1900, his government introduced a general amnesty bill.

Because it wanted to safeguard the army by diverting Dreyfusard attacks to religious orders, or because it was the price it had to pay to secure Dreyfusard support for the proposed amnesty, or because Waldeck believed that the anti-Republican congregations posed a real threat, or because of all these things, the government took action against the most violent among them. A government decree dissolved the Assumptionist

Fathers, who sponsored the virulent and anti-Semitic (and anti-Protestant and anti-Freemason) newspaper *La Croix*. The order had involved itself in politics by vigorously supporting anti-Dreyfusard candidates. The Augustinian order was similarly dissolved, and other religious orders were required to seek government authorization. But implementation of the Associations Act embodying this requirement was left to Waldeck's successor, Emile Combes, who took a harsher line and opened the door to separation of church and state in 1905.

Socially conservative, Waldeck despaired over the Radical and Socialist successes in the legislative elections of 1892. Fearing that he could not work with a left-wing majority (which was to control the new Chamber of Deputies until the outbreak of World War I) and in poor health, he resigned on June 1, 1902. His government had survived for three years, a record in France's Third Republic. Waldeck-Rousseau died of cancer two years later.

Emile Zola (1840–1902)

This great French novelist who ardently defended Dreyfus. His open letter accusing the generals of conspiring to commit an injustice kept the case alive. Zola was the son of an engineer from Venice; hence, the aspersions cast on his Italian origins by anti-Dreyfusards. Although born in Paris, he spent much of his childhood in Aix-en-Provence, in southern France, where he was friendly with the future artist Paul Cézanne. In the early 1860s, Zola worked as publicity director for the Hachette publishing house and became part of the literary bohemian scene in Paris. He left to pursue a career in literature and published numerous naturalistic novels, most notably the Rougon-Macquart series between 1869 and 1893. They depicted the characters of two families—characters whose behavior was "determined" by the forces of heredity and environment. Very much a product of the scientifically oriented realist school, Zola was opposed by idealistic critics and, later, by such anti-Dreyfusard writers as Ferdinand Brunetière, Emile Faguet, and Maurice Barrès, who mustered enough strength to bar him from the *Académie Française*, the elite body of intellectuals and writers.

At the time of Dreyfus's degradation, Zola was struck by the hostility of the crowd, but like so many others, had no reason to question the guilty verdict. However, in May 1896, anticipating his subsequent enlistment in

Dreyfusard ranks, Zola was horrified by the anti-Semitism shown in a press campaign launched by Drumont and other nationalists. The previous year, an anti-Semitic deputy had submitted legislation excluding naturalized citizens, Jews, and spouses of Jews from holding public office. That April, the journal *La France Catholique* encouraged its Catholic readers to see a painting depicting a ritual murder supposedly committed by Jews. Showing his hatred of intolerance, Zola published articles in *Le Figaro* that condemned "primitive" anti-Semitic outbursts. He wrote sarcastically, "Let us devour each other because we do not shout in the same way and because our hair grows differently."[22]

Zola did not join with Dreyfusards until introduced by Scheurer-Kestner to Bernard-Lazare and Leblois, who showed him Picquart's evidence on November 13, 1897. Shaken, Zola published the first of a series of articles in *Le Figaro* that defended Scheurer-Kestner against attacks by nationalists. The subsequent loss of subscribers caused the newspaper to abandon its support of Dreyfus and deprived Zola of a platform. He resorted to publishing pamphlets warning the French of the reactionary threat posed by anti-Dreyfusards, anti-Semites, and elements within the Church. Zola believed that Catholic fanatics were eager to promote religious war, recreate a medieval theocracy, and repudiate the revolutionary tradition of liberty and equality.

After Esterhazy's acquittal and Picquart's arrest, a bleak moment for the supporters of Dreyfus, Zola resolved to break with the moderation shown by Scheurer-Kestner and Mathieu. He would make use of his worldwide reputation by bringing a lawsuit against himself and so enable the entire truth to come out in a public courtroom. He completed his open letter to the president of the Republic, and after coining the title, *"J'accuse"* (I accuse,) Clemenceau published the letter in his newspaper, *L'Aurore* (The Dawn) the morning of June 13, 1898.

Zola took advantage of his novelist's flair for the dramatic when he recounted the stages in the Affair. Deliberately opening himself to charges of libel, he accused by name the officers, war ministers, handwriting experts, and courts-martial of crimes, conspiracies, and cover-ups. The edition sold out. The Dreyfusard movement was relaunched. No longer was it a legal fight over one man's conviction but the struggle for justice against those who gave priority to the national interest and the institution (the army) entrusted with its safekeeping. The Socialist Jules Guesde called Zola's letter "the greatest revolutionary act of the century."

Nationalists and anti-Semites were livid and staged protests that escalated into full-blown riots. In Algiers, which had a sizable Jewish community, entire streets were burned out. At his trial, Zola wanted to cover the details of the Dreyfus Affair, but the court would hear only that evidence that related to whether Esterhazy's judges had received orders to acquit him. Here, adequate proof was lacking, Zola's proclamation that "the future of France was threatened by the injustice of the Dreyfus Affair and could be isolated" notwithstanding. Cowed jurors saw their names and addresses published by *La Libre Parole*. They found him guilty, and he was fined and condemned to a year's imprisonment. Although an appeals court quashed the verdict on technical grounds and ordered a second trial to be held at Versailles on July 18, it was clear that Zola would not be allowed to elaborate on all the accusations made in his letter. He was persuaded to leave for exile in England, where his pen could do more good than if he were locked in a cell.

La Civilita Cattolica, the official Jesuit review, elated, proclaimed that "the Jews invented the charge of a judicial error [and that] the real error was that [of 1789] which had granted them French nationality, a law that must be repealed." Even so, Zola's prediction that France would find herself isolated was borne out in the foreign press. For the *Chicago Tribune*, the Zola trial was "a perversion of justice." The *London Times* stated that Zola would be honored "wherever men have souls that are free." The *Berliner Tageblatt* was more cutting: "The French Army has won its first victory since the 1870 defeat."

Zola returned to France when the High Court rejected the 1894 judgment and ordered Dreyfus returned from Devil's Island for a second trial. He did not live to see Dreyfus rehabilitated. On September 30, 1902, he was found dead, in mysterious circumstances, of carbon monoxide poisoning because of a blocked chimney. At the time Dreyfus was reinstated into the army in 1906, the Chamber voted on Jaurès's proposal to transfer Zola's ashes to the Panthéon, the great repository in Paris where the most honored of the French find a final resting place. Even then, the repercussions of the Dreyfus Affair were felt: the royalist anti-Dreyfusard newspaper *L'Action Française* had called for protests, and unruly crowds gathered. Dreyfus, who had come to pay his last respects, was wounded in an assassination attempt.

Notes

1. Jean-Denis Bredin, *The Affair: The Case of Alfred Dreyfus* (New York: George Braziller, 1986), 137–138.

2. Eric Cahm, *The Dreyfus Affair in French Society and Politics* (New York: Longman, 1996), 179.

3. Michael Burns, *Dreyfus: A Family Affair, 1789–1945* (New York: HarperCollins, 1991), 120.

4. David Levering Lewis, *Prisoners of Honor: The Dreyfus Affair* (New York: Morrow, 1994), 17

5. *La Libre Parole*, May 18, 1896

6. Lewis, 196.

7. Bredin, 361.

8. Burns, 469.

9. Bredin, 380.

10. Lewis, 179.

11. Burns, 137.

12. Pierre Quillard, *Le Monument Henry* (Paris, 1899). These comments are scattered throughout the book.

13. Leslie Derfler, *Alexandre Millerand: The Socialist Years* (The Hague and Paris: Mouton, 1977), 135.

14. *Journal Officiel*, Débats, Chambre des députés, January 22, 1898

15. Lewis, 97

16. Eric Cahm, 159.

17. Lewis, 21.

18. Lewis, 133.

19. G.W. Steevens, *The Tragedy of Dreyfus* (New York: Harper and Brothers, 1899), 286.

20. Steevens, cited in Cahm, 174.

21. Bredin, 185.

22. Roderick Kedward, *The Dreyfus Affair* (London: Longmans, 1965), 82.

PRIMARY DOCUMENTS OF THE DREYFUS AFFAIR

A Traitor Is Discovered

The Dreyfus Affair began on September 27, 1894, when the covering note (the *bordereau*) listing a number of accompanying documents arrived at the Statistical (Intelligence) Section of the War Ministry in Paris. It was found in the wastebasket of the German military attaché in Paris, Lieutenant-Colonel Maximilien von Schwartzkoppen, and presumably had been sent to him. Torn in half, unsigned, and undated, it was retrieved by what the section called "the usual route"—by the cleaning woman who worked for the section, Madame Bastian. In an age before the invention of paper shredders, she regularly turned over the discarded papers of the attaché for examination. The career officer in charge at the time, Major Henry, realized the implication of the discovery—a French officer had committed treason—and accordingly informed his superiors.

Document 1
The *Bordereau*
Translated by the author

Although I had no word you wished to see me, Monsieur, I am nevertheless sending you some interesting pieces of information:

1. A note on the hydraulic brake of the 120 mm. gun and on the way the gun has performed

2. A note on the covering troops (under the revised plan some changes will be made)

3. A note on a change in artillery formations

4. A note that concerns Madagascar
5. The draft Field Artillery Firing Manual. This last document is extremely difficult to get, and I can only have it available for a very few days. The Ministry of War has distributed a fixed number of copies to the relevant corps, and the corps are responsible for them. Each officer having one must return it after maneuvers. So if you want to take what interests you from it and hold on to it for me, I will get one—unless you would like me to copy it all out and send the copy to you

I am about to leave for maneuvers.

Source: The newspaper *Le Matin* published a facsimile of the *bordereau* on November 10, 1896.

Dreyfus Is Arrested and Charged with Treason

Three of the five documents referred to in the *bordereau* involved matters of artillery. It was natural that suspicion should fall on an artillery officer assigned to the General Staff. According to Lieutenant-Colonel d'Abboville, the service's deputy chief, there were similarities between the handwriting on a standard report that Dreyfus had written previously and the handwriting of the *bordereau*. Then, when under suspicion, there seems little doubt that the captain's unpopularity and Jewish origins accounted for a presumption of guilt. To entrap Dreyfus, the interrogating officer, Major du Paty de Clam, dictated a letter to him, and after a few minutes charged him with having written the incriminating document. What follows is Dreyfus's recollection of the events that led up to the accusation of treason.

Document 2
Dreyfus's Memoirs

The year 1893 passed without incidents. My daughter Jeanne came to shed a new ray of sunshine in our home.

The year 1894 was to be the last of my service in the Second Bureau of the General Staff of the Army. During the last quarter of the year I was named for the regulation term of service in an infantry regiment stationed in Paris.

I began my term on the 1st of October. Saturday, the 13th of October, 1894, I received a service-note directing me to go the following Monday, at nine o'clock in the morning, to the Ministry of War for the general inspection. It was expressly stated that I should be in *tenue bourgeoise* (civilian dress). The hour seemed to me very early for the general inspection, which is usually passed late in the day; the mention of civilian dress surprised me as well. Still, after making these remarks while reading the note, I soon forgot them, as the matter appeared unimportant.

As was our custom, my wife and I dined on Sunday evening with her parents. We came away gay and light-hearted, as we always did after these family gatherings.

On Monday morning I left my family. My son Pierre, who was then three and a half years old and was accustomed to accompany me to the door when I went out, came with me that morning as usual. That was one of my keenest remembrances through all my misfortunes. Very often in my nights of sorrow and despair I lived over the moment when I held my child in my arms for the last time. In this recollection I always found renewed strength of purpose.

The morning was bright and cool, the rising sun driving away the thin mist; everything foretold a beautiful day. As I was a little ahead of time, I walked back and forth before the Ministry Building for a few minutes, then went upstairs. On entering the office I was received by Commandant (Major) Picquart, who seemed to be waiting for me, and who took me at once into his room. I was somewhat surprised at finding none of my comrades, as officers are always called in groups to the general inspection. After a few minutes of commonplace conversation Commandant Picquart conducted me to the private office of the Chief of General Staff. I was greatly amazed to find myself received, not by the Chief of General Staff, but by Commandant du Paty de Clam, who was in uniform. Three persons in civilian dress, who were utterly unknown to me, were also there. These three persons were M. Cochefert, *Chef de la Sûreté* (head of the secret police), his secretary, and the Keeper of the Records, M. Gribelin.

Commandant du Paty de Clam came directly toward me and said in a choking voice: "The General is coming. While waiting, I have a letter to write, and as my finger is sore, will you write it for me?" Strange as the request was under the circumstances, I at once complied. I sat down at a little table, while Commandant du Paty placed himself at my side and very near me, following my hand with his eye. After first requiring me to fill up an inspection form, he dictated to me a letter of which certain passages recalled the accusing letter that I knew afterward, and which was called the *bordereau*. In the course of his dictation the Commandant interrupted me sharply, saying: "You tremble." (I was not trembling. At the Court Martial of 1894, he explained his brusque interruption by saying that he had perceived I was not trembling under the dictation; believing therefore that he had to do with one who was simulating, he had tried in this way to shake my assurance.) The vehement remark surprised me greatly, as did the hostile attitude of Commandant Du Paty. But as all suspicion was far from my mind, I thought only that he was displeased at my writing it badly. My fingers were cold, for the temperature outside was chilly, and I had been only a few minutes in the warm room. So I answered, "My fingers are cold."

As I continued writing without any sign of perturbation, Commandant Du Paty tried a new interruption and said violently: "Pay attention; it is a grave matter." Whatever may have been my surprise at a procedure as rude as it was uncommon, I said nothing and simply applied myself to writing more carefully. Thereupon Commandant Du Paty, as he explained to the Court Martial of 1894, concluded that, my self-possession being unshakable, it was useless to push the experiment further. The scene of the dictation had been prepared in every detail; but it had not answered the expectations of those who had arranged it.

As soon as the dictation was over, Commandant du Paty arose and, placing his hand on my shoulder, cried out in a loud voice: "In the name of the law, I arrest you; you are accused of the crime of high treason." A thunderbolt falling at my feet would not have produced in me a more violent emotion; I blurted out disconnected sentences, protesting against so infamous an accusation, which nothing in my life could have given rise to.

Next, M. Cochefert and his secretary threw themselves on me and searched me. I did not offer the slightest resistance, but cried to them: "Take my keys, open everything in my house; I am innocent." Then I added, "Show me at least the proofs of the infamous act you pretend I have committed." They answered that the accusations were overwhelming, but refused to state what they were or who had made them. . . . When I found myself in that gloomy cell, still under the terrific influence of the scene I had just gone though and of the monstrous accusation brought against me, when I thought of all those whom I had left at home but a few hours before in the fullness of happiness, I fell into a state of fearful excitement and raved from grief. . . . But no matter what my tortures may have been, my conscience was awake and unerringly dictated my duty to me. "If you die," it said to me, "they will believe you guilty; whatever happens, you must live to cry aloud your innocence in the face of the world."

It was only on the fifteenth day after my arrest that Commandant du Paty showed me a photograph of the accusing letter since called the *bordereau.*

I did not write this letter, NOR WAS I IN ANY WAY RESPONSIBLE FOR IT.

Source: Alfred Dreyfus, *Five Years of My Life, 1894–1899* (New York: McClure Phillips & Co., 1901), 5–13.

The Role of the Anti-Semitic Press

Edouard Drumont was a notorious anti-Semite who had previously published a book on the "threat" to France posed by Jewish "infiltration" of the nation's institutions, particularly the army. His newspaper, *La Libre Parole*, which included army officers among its readers, was committed to stirring up anti-Jewish sentiment, and he had no doubts as to Dreyfus's guilt. It was this newspaper that broke the story of an officer's arrest for treason, pressed for the officer to be identified, and criticized the war minister for delay. In the following newspaper article, Drumont invoked a crude determinism: Dreyfus, and the Jews, cannot help but betray the country they live in because they have no country.

Document 3
The Soul of Dreyfus
(Translated by the author)

Indeed, if we consider his origins and his type, he has been simply tactless; he did in the Army what he would have done in a bank or at a racetrack: he sold information to the competition. He has abused the confidence placed in him, but he has not committed any crime against the country. In order to betray his country, he had to have one, and a country is not acquired by means of an act of naturalization. One's country is the land of one's forefathers, the land of one's ancestors: Dreyfus's ancestors were not of our land; they were everywhere wanderers and nomads, and their sons had no notion of what a fatherland meant.

Barrès [Maurice Barrés, the French novelist whose vengeful hatred of Germany, fanned by strong anti-Semitism, led him to combat all efforts to rehabilitate Dreyfus.] put it beautifully:

One understands by nation a group of men united by common legends, a tradition, customs formed in a common milieu during a more or less long series of ancestors. Naturalization is a legal fiction which allows for sharing in the advantage of a nation but which cannot give it character.

You have been criminal in relying on these strangers. To these itinerants, to those who in Rome are called *peregrini* (wanderers), you divulge your most sacred secrets. You are ridiculous in judging those who have abused your idiotic lack of foresight in the name of an ideal, traditions, conceptions, which are not theirs.

The only one who seems to me to make a little sense in this regard is Monsieur de Pontbriand, the Deputy from the Loire-Inférieure (Department). Instead of delivering melodramatic tirades, he simply suggests we learn to appreciate authority, which is a very fair request. He is going to submit a bill that would require at least three generations of French descent to qualify for public employment. The Jews risk the calamity that confronts them should they oppose this bill. They would be wrong, and it is not as an enemy that I advise them to accept a measure that will gradually acclimatize them.

There is something more powerful than all the Parisian worthies, than all the campaigns of a subsidized press, than all the maneuvers of Jewdom. There is the inevitable and invincible resistance of the nation itself, the very soul of France. In insisting on imposing themselves on us, in imprudently claiming to be the equal of those who create the French nation, the Jews are preparing with their own hands the most fearful catastrophe of their tragic history....

When *Jewish France* (Drumont's book) was published, Zaddoc-Kahn [the Grand Rabbi of Paris] was told, "It is a pamphlet."

"No," he replied, "it is a prophecy. . . ."

Jewish France appeared in 1886. Eight years is not much time for an idea to take root. . . .

Lord, I do not take pride in this accomplishment. Of all men I have always been the weakest, the most sentimental, the most easy to discourage, and it is you who have given me the courage to awake my country. Protect me, oh Lord! . . .

This is what I have to say to all those who have encouraged and congratulated me, to those who were warned against me and who now acknowledged that I was right, and especially to our young friends in the anti-Semitic groups that have surfaced almost everywhere, in Paris, in Lyons, in Dijon, in Montpellier.

My books will have rendered an immense service to our dear France in exposing the Jewish peril, in preventing her from being delivered bound hand and foot to the enemy, ambushed in wartime in all the important agencies by the Dreyfusses and Reinachs. I am happy to have written these books, but I do not deserve praise because I could not help but write them. A higher will said to me, "Speak!" I have spoken.

Source: La Libre Parole, December 26, 1894.

Dreyfus Is Degraded

Having been court-martialed, found guilty, and sentenced to deportation, Dreyfus faced a further humiliation: degradation, the formal ceremony in which he would literally be stripped of his rank and paraded before a detachment of troops and the public specifically convened for that purpose. The generals would have preferred that he commit suicide, and Dreyfus considered the prospect. But he wrote to his wife, "I must live. I must marshal all my strength to wash away the stain on the name of my honor. . . . Our honor is everything." By 9 A.M. on the scheduled day, the crowd numbered several thousand. Many believed in his guilt and so despised the "traitor." For the readers of Drumont's *La Libre Parole*, the ceremony would mark the end of the invidious Jewish attempt to infiltrate the army and bring down the nation. For them, Dreyfus's degradation was "a precondition of national regeneration."

Document 4
Dreyfus Recalls His Degradation

The degradation took place Saturday, the 5th of January (1895). I underwent the horrible torture without weakness.

Before the ceremony, I waited for an hour in the hall of the garrison adjutant at the Ecole Militaire, guarded by the captain of gendarmes [militarized security police], Lebrun-Renault. During these long minutes I gathered up all the forces of my being. The memory of the dreadful months which I had just passed came back to me, and in broken sentences I recalled to the captain the last visit which Commandant du Paty de Clam had made to me in my prison. I protested against the vile acusation which had been brought against me; I recalled that I had written again to the Minister to tell him of my innocence. . . .

After this I was marched to the centre of the square, under a guard of four men and a corporal.

Nine o'clock struck. General Darras, commanding the parade, gave the order to carry arms.

I suffered agonizingly, but held myself erect with all my strength. To sustain me I called up the memory of my wife and children.

As soon as the sentence had been read out, I cried aloud, addressing myself to the troops:

"Soldiers, they are degrading an innocent man. Vive la France, vive l'armée"! (Long live France, long live the army!)

A sergeant of the Republican Guard came up to me. He tore off rapidly buttons, trousers-stripes, the signs of my rank from cap and sleeves, and then broke my sword across his knee. I saw all these material emblems of my honor fall at my feet. Then, my whole being racked by a fearful paroxysm, but with body erect and head high, I shouted again and again to the soldiers and to the assembled crowed the cry of my soul.

"I am innocent!"

The parade continued. I was compelled to make the whole round of the square. I heard the howls of a deluded mob, I felt the thrill which I knew must be running through those people, since they believed that before them was a convicted traitor to France; and I struggled to transmit to their hearts another thrill,—belief in my innocence.

The round of the square made, the torture would be over, I believed.

But the agony of that long day was only beginning.

Source: Alfred Dreyfus, *Five Years of My Life, 1894–1899* (New York: McClure Phillips & Co., 1901), 49–51

Picquart Confronts His Superiors

When Picquart was named the new head of the Statistical Section, his predecessor, Colonel Sandherr, told him that the chief of staff, General

Boisdeffre, was still worried about the Dreyfus case. Boisdeffre himself told Picquart that "the Jews would not let it rest" and that he should continue to "feed the file." Thus, when the fragments of a special delivery letter came to the section, the famous *petit-bleu*—a letter written to Esterhazy but never sent, by Schwartzkoppen, Picquart suspected another traitor and launched an investigation of Esterhazy. When his investigation convinced him that Esterhazy, not Dreyfus, had written the *bordereau*, he completed a lengthy report in early September stating the evidence in support of his conclusions. Neither the chief nor the deputy chief of staff, General Gonse, encouraged him; they rather insisted on keeping "the two affairs" separate. When on September 15 Picquart told Gonse he wanted to arrest Esterhazy, to his astonishment the latter exploded: "What difference does it make if that Jew is on Devil's Island?" and "If you keep still, no one will ever know." Picquart replied that it was "abominable" for an innocent man to suffer so and that although he did not know what he would do, "I will not take the secret to the grave with me." What follows is Picquart's report to the minister of justice and his recollection of his meeting with General Gonse. Although written two years after his first reports, it admirably sums up the findings of 1896.

Document 5
Picquart's Report

Paris, September 14, 1898

Sir,

I have the honor to indicate to you three reasons upon which I base my deep and firm conviction of the innocence of Dreyfus:

First, I give a summary of these reasons; I shall pass later to the detailed development of each of them in turn.

I. Dreyfus was arrested solely upon the suspicion of having written the *bordereau*. When the *bordereau* came into the hands of the bureau of information, it was supposed *a priori* and unjustly, that, in view of the documents enumerated therein, it could have been written only by an officer of the Ministry, preferably by an artillery officer, and the handwritings of the officers of the General Staff were compared with that of the *bordereau*. . . .

The writing of the *bordereau* bears merely a resemblance to that of Dreyfus. On the other hand, it is identical with that of Esterhazy. The documents specified in the *bordereau* are, as a rule, of no small value. Dreyfus, had he been inclined to treason, could have supplied himself much more. Moreover, the documents in question bear no relation to the particular ones which Dreyfus had in hand at the time the *bordereau* was written. . . .

II. When Dreyfus was arrested, in an attempt to lend his *dossier* more weight, a secret *dossier* was made up, and this was communicated to the judges of the court martial. Not one of these documents is applicable to Dreyfus. . . .

When, by order of General de Boisdeffre I went on September 3, 1896 to report to General Gonse the report of my inquiry on the subject of Esterhazy and Dreyfus, the General listened to my reasons and did not dispute them. He merely made a face and said to me, "Well then, we have been mistaken!" Then he instructed me not to concern myself with this matter. The letter of September, 1896, shows clearly that he brought forward no affirmation adverse to mine. At the time of his return to Paris on September 15th, he was still more explicit. I think I can repeat word for word the conversation I had with him on this subject, and which will never be effaced from my memory.

The General: What business is it of yours if this Jew is on the *Ile du Diable*?

R: But if he is innocent?

G: How do you expect to go all over this trial again? It would be the most shocking story. General Mercier and General Saussier [the military governor of Paris] are both tangled up in it.

R: But, General, he is innocent, and that should be enough to revise the case. But, from another point of view, you know that his family are at work. They are searching everywhere for the true culprit, and if they find him, what will be our position?

G: If you say nothing, no one will ever know.

R: General, what you say is contemptible. I do not know what I shall do, but in any event I shall not allow this secret to be buried with me. And I left him instantly. From that moment I understood clearly the situation. . . .

Source: G. W. Steevens, *The Tragedy of Dreyfus* (New York: Harper & Brothers, 1899), 280–286

The Affair Becomes Ideological

After Esterhazy's acquittal, the Dreyfusard cause reached its lowest ebb. Emile Zola then decided to break with the moderate and legalistic tactics until then pursued and ensure that the case, with all its deceit and lies, would be revealed to the public. This could be done in a civil courtroom, and so Zola deliberately courted a libel suit. His open letter to the president of the Republic was published in Clemenceau's newspaper, *L'Aurore* (The Dawn), the morning of January 13, 1898, under the huge headline across the front page, *"J'accuse"* (I accuse). After recounting the sequence of events and demonstrating that the indictment of Dreyfus was based on only the *bordereau*, his letter concluded with the specific accusations, which prompted the title given to the document by Clemenceau. It is those accusations that follow.

Document 6
Emile Zola's "*J'accuse*"
(Translated by the author)

. . . So I repeat, even more vehemently than before, that truth is on the march and nothing will stop it. The Affair has only now begun because only now are the positions clear; on the one hand, the guilty who do not want to see justice done; on the other, those who seek justice and will give their lives to see that it is carried out. I said it before and I repeat it now, truth buried in the earth grows and swells, and when it explodes it blows everything up with it. Only time will tell whether we have prepared for the most resounding disaster.

But this letter is long, Mister President, and it is time to bring it to an end:

I accuse Lieutenant Colonel du Paty de Clam of having been the diabolic creator of a judicial error, unknowingly, I would like to believe, and of having then defended his evil creation for the past three years by the most absurd and blameworthy machinations.

I accuse General Mercier of having made himself an accomplice, if for no other reason than because of mental incapacity, in one of the greatest crimes of the century.

I accuse General Billot of having held in his hands the absolute proof of Dreyfus's innocence and of having concealed it, of having made himself guilty of a crime against humanity and against justice for political purposes and in order to save the compromised General Staff.

I accuse Generals de Boisdeffre and Gonse of having made themselves accomplices in the same crime, one no doubt because of his impassioned clericalism, the other, perhaps, by that *esprit de corps* which makes the War Office the holy Ark, unattackable.

I accuse General de Pellieux and Major Ravary of having carried out a villainous investigation, by which I mean the most monstrously biased investigation whose own report creates for us an imperishable document of naive audacity.

I accuse the three handwriting experts, Messrs. Belhomme, Varinard, and Courd of having submitted deceitful and fraudulent reports, unless a medical examination reveals deficiencies in their vision and judgment.

I accuse the War Office of having waged an abominable press campaign, particularly in *L'Eclair* and *L'Echo de Paris*, to mislead public opinion and conceal their misdeeds.

Finally, I accuse the first Court-Martial of having broken the law by condemning a defendant on the strength of a single document, and I accuse the second Court-Martial [Esterhazy's] of having followed orders to cover up that illegality by committing, in turn, the juridical crime of knowingly acquitting a guilty man.

In making these accusations, I am aware that I am liable under Articles 30 and 31 of the Law of 29 July 1881 relating to the press, which punishes acts of defamation. I am willingly exposing myself to that law.

As for the people I am accusing, I do not know them, I have never met them, and I bear them no bitterness or hatred. They are only entities, embodiments of social wrongdoing. And the act I am performing here is only a revolutionary means to hasten the explosion of truth and justice.

I have only one passion, to shed light in the name of humanity, which has suffered so and which has a right to happiness. My fiery protest is no more than the cry of my soul. Let them dare, then, to bring me to the Court of Appeal, and let an inquiry be held in the light of day!

I am waiting.

Mister President, please accept the assurance of my deepest respect.

Source: L'Aurore, January 13, 1898. Zola's letter, especially its concluding accusations, may be found in numerous histories of the Affair (see, for example, that of Joseph Reinach, *Histoire de l'Affaire Dreyfus,* [Paris: La Revue blanche, 1901–1911], 3:228–229) and on the Internet sites listed in the Annotated Bibliography.

The Anti-Semitic Outburst

A renewal of anti-Semitic agitation broke out in the wake of the Zola letter. The day after its publication, 3,000 young people paraded in Nantes, smashing the windows of Jewish shops and trying to break into the synagogue. Homes of Jewish professors were attacked in Rennes. Crowds in Bordeaux shouted, "Death to the Jews," "Death to Zola," and "Death to Dreyfus." Similar scenes were observed in other provincial cities. Police and troops had to be sent to stop the pillaging. Rioting lasted six days in Rouen, five in Bordeaux and Marseilles, and somewhat less elsewhere. The greatest outburst took place in Algeria, then incorporated into France, whose population of 320,000 included over 50,000 Jews. Riots in all the major cities, and particularly in Algiers, lasted several days. Jewish neighborhoods were set ablaze, and no Jewish shop escaped damage. Several Jews were stoned, and one was bludgeoned to death. Hordes of demonstrators took to the streets singing anti-Semitic songs. Two of these songs follow.

Document 7
Anti-Semitic Songs

"Marche Antisémite"

A mort les Juifs! A mort les Juifs!
Il faut les pendre
Sans plus attendre
A mort les Juifs! A mort les Juifs!
Il faut les pendre
Par le fif!

"Anti-Semitic March"

Death to the Jews! Death to the Jews!
We must hang them
Without further delay
Death to the Jews! Death to the Jews!
We must hang them
By the nose!

"Marseillaise Antijuive"

Il y a trop longtemps qu'nous
  sommes dans la misère,
Chassons l'étranger,
Ca i'ra travalier;
Ce qu'il nous faut, c'est un meilleur
  salaire,
Chassons de notre pays,
Toute cette sale bande de joudis!

"Anti-Jewish Marseillaise"

We have lived in misery too long,

Let's chase out the foreigner,
That'll give us work;
What we need is a better salary,

Let's chase out of our country,
The filthy band of Kikes!

Source: Jean-Denis Bredin, *The Affair: The Case of Alfred Dreyfus* (New York: George Braziller, 1986), 287–288

Socialist Neutrality

The origins of socialism are deeply rooted in French history, but only in the last decades of the nineteenth century did it emerge as a modern organized political movement. While the repression of the Paris Commune in 1871 held back its growth, that same repression encouraged the domination of the Marxist variety, at the expense of other factions. In 1893, over forty Socialists were elected to the Chamber of Deputies, and they became a force to be reckoned with. But at the outset of the Dreyfus Affair, the drive to reopen the case and the opposition it met seemed to Socialists to define a struggle between two bourgeois groups struggling for political supremacy. For many Socialists and their largely working-class constituents, labor experienced greater injustices than that inflicted on a rich army officer by his peers. After initially criticizing the government for the leniency shown an officer convicted of treason (Would not an enlisted man have received the death penalty? they wondered.), most Socialists followed the example of neutrality set in the Boulanger and Panama affairs. In mid-January 1898, thirty-three socialist deputies signed a manifesto calling on party members and labor "to remain aloof" from bourgeois struggles. Those now invoking the cause of human rights and individual dignity had stolen from workers all the guarantees claimed for Dreyfus. Their manifesto of neutrality follows.

Document 8
The Manifesto of the Socialist Deputies
(Translated by the author)

Citizens:

Because of all the agitation spawned by the Dreyfus Affair, obscurity has thickened relentlessly and men of good will are painfully seeking their way. Above all, the socialist proletariat is in need of clarity. We do not have the capacity to pass judgment on the very heart of the Dreyfus Affair. In contemporary society where so many forces are ranged against truth and justice, it is impossible for us to recognize, in principle, the authority of the rendered judgment. Nor do we have any particular reason to reject or respect the specific judgments rendered in this Affair. The day before yesterday we even voted our support for a former Minister of War who said that we should accept the legitimacy of the document he showed us, a document that according to him could suddenly overwhelm Dreyfus's supporters and establish the latter's culpability.

It was the ministerial majority, a majority of the center and of the right, that opposed him. Without passing judgment on the heart of the matter, we only ask for clarification.

Why has the Dreyfus Affair taken on such vast dimensions? Because it has become a battleground of the two rival factions of the bourgeois class, the two bourgeois classes: the Opportunists and the clericals. Opportunists and clericals alike work to deceive the democratic process and bring it to heel. They both seek to keep the people in tutelage, to crush the workers' unions, to prolong by all possible means the capitalist and wage-earning regime, and to assure their own privileged class the unrestrained exploitation of labor and budgetary matters.

However, they quarrel over the division of their social gains and they wrangle over the exploitation of the Republic and the people, as did the barbaric clans who set out to plunder and who fought each other over the spoils. The Dreyfus Affair provided the two clans with the pretext to join battle. On one side the clericals, suddenly brought closer to power thanks to the treason of the republicans, seeking places and emoluments with a lust whetted by a fifteen-year fast. They would like to exploit the sentence of treason against one Jew to disqualify all Jews, together with all dissidents, Protestants, and free-thinkers. They would thus deprive all their rivals of important administrative and judicial posts. . . . All these men twist words out of their really national context, cry "France for the French," which for them means "France for us and us alone. All the prey for our long teeth." And on the other side, the Jewish capitalists, who after all the scandals which have discredited them need to keep their part of the plunder to rehabilitate themselves, at least in part. If they succeed in demonstrating that one of their own was subject to a judicial error and public prejudice, they would seek, in the direct rehabilitation of an individual belonging to their own clan and in accord with their opportunistic allies, the indirect rehabilitation of the entire Jewish and Panamist group.

In the convulsive struggle of two rival bourgeois factions, everything is hypocrisy, everything is fraudulent. The clericals lie when they describe their shameful appetite for positions and rewards. The Opportunists lie when to save themselves they invoke the human rights they themselves previously violated.

Citizens, raise your hearts above this ignominious conflict. Proletarians, do not enlist on either side of this bourgeois civil war. . . . Do not let yourselves be divided by these incomplete and contradictory words. Shout your triple cry of war: War on Jewish or Christian capital, war on clericalism, war on military oligarchy.

Source: La Petite République, January 20, 1898.

Jaurès Comes to the Defense of Dreyfus

The great voice opposing neutrality was now that of Jean Jaurès. Defeated in the 1898 election, he threw himself into editorial work on the socialist newspaper *La Petite République*. Once convinced of Dreyfus's innocence, he viewed the Affair not as a simple struggle over the guilt of an officer or even one between two rival bourgeois factions but as between the progressive elements in the Republic and the organized forces of reaction. During the summer of 1898, he wrote a series of articles, *Les Preuves* (The Evidence), to demonstrate Dreyfus's innocence. Although, Jaurès, together with other Socialists, had argued that what happened within a bourgeois republic made little difference to the working population of the country, he now came to identify the cause of individual liberty, which transcended the perceived "national interest," with the democratic Republic. He broke with the signers of the manifesto (many, but not all, of whom would be persuaded to defend Dreyfus only after Henry's confession, when it was politically expedient to do so), and in this series of cutting articles he underscored the weakness of the army's case. In showing that it was in their own interests to do so and in revealing his own humanistic vision of Socialist thought, he was to complete the process of bringing French socialism to the defense of the Republic. The following selection is from the first of Jaurès's articles.

Document 9
Jaurès Presents His Evidence
(*Translated by the author*)

Today we socialists have the right to set out against all the rulers who for years have fought us in the name of the principles of the French Revolution.

We cry out to them: "What have you done to the Declaration of the Rights of Man and to individual liberty? You have made them suspect; you have sacrificed them to the insolence of military power. You are the renegades of the bourgeois revolution."

Yes, I know. I hear the contradictions pointed to by our enemies. *La Libre Parole* tells us sweetly, "Here are socialists, revolutionaries, who are preoccupied with legality."

I have only one word in response. There are two parts to capitalist and bourgeois legality. There is a collection of laws designed to safeguard the basic injustice in our society; there are laws that consecrate the privileges of capitalist ownership, the exploitation of wage earners by the possessing classes. We want to bring an end to these laws, even by revolution if necessary, to abolish capitalist legality in order to give rise to a new order. But alongside these laws of privilege and rapine, enacted by and for a particular class, there are others that sum up the limited progress of humanity, the modest guarantees little by little won by lengthy effort over the course of centuries and during the lengthy aftermath of revolutionary activity.

Perhaps the most important among these laws is that which does not permit a man to be condemned without allowing him to defend himself. Opposed to the nationalists who wish to retain of bourgeois legality all that which preserves capital, and surrender to the generals all that which protects the individual, we revolutionary socialists seek within the existing legal system the abolition of the capitalist portion and the preservation of the human portion. We defend legal rights against the noncommissioned officers who want to end them, just as we would defend, if necessary, republican legality against putschist [putsch is German for uprising] generals.

Yes, I am well aware that amongst us there are comrades who say: "This does not concern a proletarian; let the bourgeoisie fight it out amongst themselves." And one of them added that phrase which, I must admit, pained me: "If it were a question of a workingman, it would be a long time before any of them would care."

I can reply that if Dreyfus had been illegally condemned, and if, in fact, as I will presently demonstrate, he is innocent, he is no longer an officer or a bourgeois: because of excessive misfortune he is stripped of all class characteristics; he is no less than humanity itself displaying the highest degree of misery and despair that one can imagine.

If he has been condemned in violation of every law, if he has been falsely condemned, it is mockery to include him among the privileged. No, he no longer belongs to that army which, by a criminal error, has degraded him. He no longer belongs to the ruling class, which because of the cowardice born of ambition hesitates to restore legality and truth to him. He is only an example of the most poignant human suffering. He is the living witness to a military lie, to political cowardice, to the crimes of those in authority.

Without contradicting our principles and without betraying the class struggle, we can certainly listen to the cry our pity evokes; we can retain human compassion in the revolutionary struggle; we are not required to leave humanity behind in order to remain socialists.

Dreyfus himself, falsely and criminally condemned by the society we fight against, whatever his origins and whatever his future, becomes a penetrating protest against the social order. By the failure of the society that persists in maintaining the violence, lies, and crimes directed against him, he becomes an element of revolution.

That is how I can reply; and I can add that as for the socialists who do wish to burrow into the depths of the shameful and criminal secrets contained in this affair, if they are not concerned with a worker, they are concerned *with the entire working class.*

Who is today most threatened by the arbitrariness of the generals, by the perpetually glorified violence of military repression? Who? The proletariat. Accordingly, it has a primary interest in punishing and discouraging the illegality and violence of courts-martial before they become a kind of commonly accepted routine. It is in the proletariat's highest interest to precipitate the moral disrepute and collapse of that reactionary army elite, which is prepared to crush it tomorrow.

Because this time the army chiefs, misguided by clannish struggles, applied their regime of arbitrariness and lies to a son of the bourgeoisie, bourgeois society is deeply disturbed and shaken, and we must profit from this agitation to diminish the moral force and the aggressive capacity of these retrograde General Staffs, which pose a direct threat to the proletariat.

It is not, therefore, to benefit humanity alone, it is to directly benefit the working class to protest, as we are doing, the clearly demonstrated illegality of the Dreyfus case. . . .

Source: La Petite République, August 10, 1898.

The Death of Henry

Following War Minister Cavaignac's speech of July 7, 1898, to the Chamber of Deputies, the speech in which he referred to documents that "incontestably" demonstrated Dreyfus's guilt, Picquart wrote to him the next day stating that two of Cavaignac's documents were irrelevant and the third, that viewed as offering "absolute proof," was a forgery. Was it Picquart's letter that prompted Cavaignac to order a subordinate to reexamine the documents? Was it the resentment expressed by both the Italian and German governments at the rejection of their repeated denials of ever having employed Dreyfus? In any event, when "the absolute proof" was placed under a strong lamp, the forgery became clear. Cavaignac interrogated Henry, who broke down and confessed. He was taken to Mont-Valérien fortress, locked in a cell in the officers' wing, and found dead the next day, an apparent suicide. Questions were raised at the time: What in the examination of the documents pointed to Henry as the forger? Exactly what had he confessed to forging: one document or more in the voluminous dossier compiled on Dreyfus? Certainly his death proved convenient for his superiors insofar as it limited the prospects for subsequent investigations into additional forgeries. Before leaving for prison, Henry had confided to his wife that his superiors had all abandoned him. Still, even the anti-Dreyfusard journalist Charles Maurras admitted that during the evening preceding his death, Henry had been drinking heavily. He had removed all his clothes. With two strokes of a razor, he had slit his throat, and the razor was found clenched in his hand. With Boisdeffre's resignation, the loss of authority by Gonse, and Esterhazy's dismissal, the conspiracy to inculpate Dreyfus appeared doomed. Following is the official letter sent by the military commanders of Mont-Valérien to the military governor of Paris, General Saussier.

Document 10
Henry Is Dead
(Translated by the author)

Mont-Valérien, 31 August, 1898

The undersigned, Walter, Artillery Major, Weapons Commander at Mont-Valérien; Varlot, Lieutenant of the Republican Guard, Senior Officer at the Paris Garrison; Fète, Lieutenant in the Sixteenth Battalion of the

Foot-Artillery, are gathered today at eight-thirty in the evening, in the room occupied by Lieutenant-Colonel Henry, Head of the Intelligence Service of the Ministry of War, currently under arrest at the Mont-Valérien fortress.

They have certified that Lieutenant-Colonel Henry was lying on his bed, after having cut his throat with a razor that was still grasped in his right hand.

The doctor called to certify the death had not yet arrived.

The body was cold, although that had already been established by the Weapons Commander.

Lieutenant-Colonel Henry had to have committed suicide about three in the afternoon.

Two letters were found on the table, one sealed, addressed to Madame Henry, and one open, containing incoherent words.

Moreover, in the pockets of his clothing, there was found a letter addressed to Mister J. Henry, 13, avenue Duquesne, and a visiting card.

All these objects were entrusted to Lieutenant Varlot to hand over to the General commanding the Paris garrison.

Finally, a wallet containing a note of 100 francs, an identity card, and some calling cards have also been sent to Mister Varlot, together with Lieutenant-Colonel Henry's change purse and watch.

The change purse contains 265 francs.

Aside from these objects, no papers have been found in Lieutenant-Colonel Henry's room or in his clothing.

Mont-Valérien, 31 August, 1898
Walter, Varlot, Fète

Source: Joseph Reinach, *Histoire de l'Affaire Dreyfus* (Paris: Fasquelle, 1902–1911), .
4: 619–620.

The Henry Memorial Fund

Few could remain neutral after Colonel Henry's confession. General Boisdeffre, the chief of staff, resigned, and the Affair seemed at an end. However, it was far from over. To the astonishment of Dreyfusards, nationalists and anti-Semites regarded both confession and suicide as acts of courage. They accepted the version put forward in their newspapers, which insisted that Henry's patriotism had prevented him from revealing the true documents, for their disclosure implicated the German emperor himself and would probably lead to war. His "patriotic forgery" was intended to save the army. The nationalist newspaper writer Charles Maurras said he "sacrificed himself . . . for the public good." Because Joseph Reinach had charged Henry with conspiring with Esterhazy, he had been sued for libel by Henry's widow. To show their support for her husband's courageous act and help her defray legal costs, Drumont and *La Libre Parole* opened a fund on behalf of the "widow and orphan against the Jew Reinach" and asked for donations. Among the many contributors were 300 Catholic priests, whose comments were recorded and published. Anticlericals used these entries to attack the entire church as anti-Semitic and anti-Dreyfusard (although there were about 50,000 priests in the country and clearly most did not contribute). Note that *abbé* is French for priest.

Document 11
The Henry Memorial Fund
(Translated by the author)

[Contributor and accompanying comment]	Francs	Centimes
Collot (L'Abbé) from Lorraine and Prisoner of the Prussians who shows confidence in the verdict of military justice and five Ministers of War	5	
Cros (L'Abbé), ex-lieutenant, for a bedside rug made of the skins of Yids, to be trampled on morning and evening	5	
Favier (L'Abbé), who hopes that God will soon avenge France	5	
Galey (L'Abbé), for the defense of eternal right against the histrionics of the Puritans and the deceit of the Jew-Huguenots	5	
Lajaire (L'Abbé de), long live the army	10	
Lamy (E. Prêtre [priest]), for the defense of a child of France	1	
Mancuert (Abbé) and M. *Gely à Pesac [Gironde]*, Two admirers of beautiful campaign against our true enemies	1	20
C. *(Abbé)*, The blood of Colonel Henry cries for vengeance	3	

[Contributor and accompanying comment]	Francs	Centimes
E.B. Paris, A priest convinced of the perversity of the Jews		50
A Country Priest, who most ardently wishes for the extermination of the two enemies of France: the Jew and the Freemason	5	
A priest from the Bayeux diocese, Down with republicans of all kind; Yids, Huguenots, Freemasons, and all who have been Judaized by them	1	
A small priest from Poitiers, who will gladly sing a requiem for the last of the Yids	1	
Three priests, Frenchmen of France who would like to put their thirty fingers on the filthy face of the Jew Reinach	3	
A very poor priest, for the widow of the soldier assassinated by the Jews	1	

Source: Pierre Quillard, *Le Monument Henry* (Paris: Stock, 1899), 94–104.

The Rennes Trial: A Second Court-Martial

Returned from Devil's Island in June 1899, Dreyfus faced a second court-martial. Deliberately placed in the provincial town of Rennes, away from Paris, it met from August 7 to September 9. Because of the numerous reporters from around the world, the event was well covered. Dreyfus, showing the suffering he had endured, testified on his own behalf. The generals and ministers of war, past and present, continued to insist on his guilt. According to French rules of law, witnesses could state beliefs, opinions, and prejudices, and confrontations between Mercier and Dreyfus and Mercier and former President Casimir-Périer took place. An attempted assassination of Dreyfus's lawyer, Labori, added to the drama. Both Labori and his colleague Demange repudiated the testimony of the generals and handwriting experts and led the defense witnesses to prove that Esterhazy had written the *bordereau*, all to no avail. Five of the seven military judges found Dreyfus once more guilty, although now with "extenuating circumstances." The following selection is part of the account of the trial by an American reporter, G. W. Steevens.

Document 12
A Reporter's Account of the Rennes Trial

The trial was to begin at half-past six. It wanted a quarter of an hour of the time when a line of mounted gendarmes, pushing the crowd out of the neighboring streets, proclaimed that they were taking Dreyfus across the road from the military prison to the High School, in whose lecture hall he was to be arraigned.

A moment later the line opened, and the crowd of journalists, waving their passes pushed through. They jammed in at a narrow door, up stone steps, though another doorway, round a corner, inside a cordon of infantry, and they were in the court. It was a lofty, oblong, buff-plastered hall larger than the Prince's Restaurant, smaller than St. James's Hall [a London restaurant and music hall in the 1890s]. With large windows on each side— square in the lower tier, circular in the upper—it was almost as light as the day outside. . . .

The Press stampeded and trampled over the matchboard [flooring], and in the fulness of time sorted itself into its appointed places. The general public shifted and scrunched behind the barrier. The center of the hall began to fill up with witnesses, with officers of infantry in red pantaloons and gunners in black. Behind the daïs appeared a sprinkling of selected spectators. Then, on the waxing bustle of the hall, came in men in black gowns with little white-edged tippets and white bands, with queer high black caps like birettas. Now we should see. And next moment—it was already half past seven—there was a hoarse cry from behind—present arms—rattle—and there filed in the seven officers in whose hands rests the conscience of France. The President—a small but soldierly man in eyeglasses, with black hair and a small face, a huge white moustache and imperial—saluted and sat down. Bring in the accused.

Instantly the black, rippling hall is still as marble, silent as the grave. A sergeant usher went to a door—the tramp of his feet was almost startling—on the right hand of the top of the hall. It opened and two officers stepped out. One of them was the greatest villain or the greatest victim in France—and for the moment men wondered which was he. It seemed almost improper that the most famous man in the world was walking in just as you or I might.

Then all saw him, and the whole hall broke into a gasp. There came in a little old man—an old, old man of thirty-nine. A middle-statured, thick-set old man in the black uniform of the artillery; over the red collar his hair was gone white as silver, and on the temples and at the back of the crown he was bald. As he turned to face the judges there was a glimpse of a face both burned and pale—a rather broad, large featured face with a thrusting jaw and chin. It was not Jewish in expression until you saw it in profile. The eyes under the glasses were set a trifle close together, and not wholly sympathetic either; you might guess him hard, stubborn, cunning. But this is only guessing: what we did see in the face was suffering and effort—a misery hardly to be borne and a tense, agonized striving to bear and to hide it. Here is a man, you would say, who has endured things unendurable, and just lives through—maybe to endure more.

He walked up two steps to his seat with a gait full of resolve yet heavy, constrained, mechanical—such a gait as an Egyptian mummy might walk with if it came to life in its swathing grave-clothes. He saluted the President with a white-gloved hand, took off his *képi* [cap], sat down. An officer of gendarmes followed and sat down beside him. The recorder, rising from beside the prosecuting officer, read out the general order constituting the court; the white moustache twitched as the President, in a small voice, put a question to the prisoner. Another sudden stillness; then came the voice of Dreyfus. No one heard what he said—thin, sapless, split, it was such as might rustle from the lips of a corpse.

What he said was, "Alfred Dreyfus: Captain of Artillery: thirty-nine years." With these three common phrases he broke the silence of four and a half years. . . .

Source: G. W. Steevens, *The Tragedy of Dreyfus*, (London: Harper and Brothers, 1899), 41–44

Dreyfus Is Pardoned

The decision of the Rennes court-martial to find Dreyfus guilty but with extenuating circumstances (the contradiction was apparent: how can an act of high treason have extenuating circumstances?) created the problem of how to carry out the sentence. Should Dreyfus be returned to Devil's Island? Should he be required to undergo another degradation ceremony? Mathieu feared his brother would not survive another prison term, and Alfred himself said, "They will have to take me by force." Waldeck-Rousseau was determined not to enforce the sentence but was reminded by War Minister Galliffet that the army would take exception to an acquittal by the High Court. What would result from a clash between the army (and the majority of the population who supported it) and the Dreyfusards (supported by international public opinion)? The military judges themselves subsequently asked that no military degradation ceremony take place—and implicitly suggested a pardon. Above all, the prime minister sought the speedy restoration of public order. When Joseph Reinach suggested that an immediate pardon would negate the military judgment, Mathieu quickly agreed. Clemenceau and Bernard-Lazare initially opposed it but were won over. Responding to Galliffet's request for a pardon, President Loubet signed the decree. In his report to Loubet, Galliffet stated the reasons for the proposed pardon: Dreyfus's renunciation of his right to appeal (which on technical grounds might have led to yet another, third, guilty verdict), his poor state of health, and the country's need for reconciliation and pacification.

Galliffet's report and proposed decree for Loubet to sign follow.

Document 13
Galliffet Asks for a Pardon
(Translated by the author)

Ministry of War
Report to the President of the French Republic
Paris, September 19, 1899

Mister President:

On September 9, the Court-Martial at Rennes, by a five to two vote, condemned Dreyfus to ten years' imprisonment: a majority vote also granted extenuating circumstances.

After having been brought before an examining board, Dreyfus withdrew his right to appeal.

The judgment became definitive, and consequently he acknowledged the legal authority before which we all must submit. The highest function of government is to have juridical decrees respected, without distinction and without ulterior motives. Resolved to fulfil this obligation, it must also show concern for that which clemency and the national interest require. The very verdict of the Court-Martial, which has acknowledged extenuating circumstances, and the quickly voiced desire that the sentence be reduced provide additional indicators that require our attention. . . .

If we deduct from the ten years of detention the five years served on Devil's Island—and we cannot do otherwise—Dreyfus will have undergone five years of deportation, and he will have to undergo five years of detention. We may ask whether it is not possible to include the deportation in the imprisonment, and in that case he would have almost completely served his sentence. The law apparently does not allow it, and it follows that Dreyfus must serve a greater penalty than that to which he was condemned.

Moreover, according to the information we have, the health of the condemned man has been seriously compromised, and that his ability to survive a prolonged imprisonment is gravely threatened.

In addition to these considerations, which evoke our solicitude, another, of a more general nature, leads to the same conclusion: a higher political interest, the need always faced by governments to recover all their energies after difficult crises and in special circumstances to resort to measures of clemency and amnesty. The government, in the opinion of a country anxiously seeking pacification, would respond poorly if, by the acts of which it is capable, whether by its own or by parliamentary initiative, it does not attempt to remove all the traces of a painful conflict.

It is up to us, Mister President, by an act of great humanity, to give the first sign of this work of appeasement that is demanded by public opinion and is required for the well-being of the Republic.

This is why I have the honor of asking you to sign the enclosed decree.

Please accept, Mr. President, the acknowledgment of my respectful devotion.

> The Minister of War
> General Galliffet
> Decree

The President of the French Republic, based on the report of the Minister of War, in view of the Law of 25 February, 1875 and in view of the opinion of the Keeper of the Seals, the Minister of Justice, decrees:

First Article: Alfred Dreyfus is forgiven the remainder of the ten years' imprisonment sentence given him by the decree of the Rennes Court-Martial, dated September 9, 1899, as well as that of military degradation.

Article 2: The Minister of War is responsible for carrying out this decree.

Signed in Paris, 19 September, 1899

Emile Loubet

For the President of the Republic,

General Galliffet

Source: Joseph Reinach, *Histoire de l'Affaire Dreyfus* (Paris: Fasquelle, 1902–1911), 5: 82–84.

The Dreyfusards Versus The Dreyfus Family

The decision to accept the pardon caused considerable dissension among the Dreyfusards. The decision to accept an amnesty brought about the disintegration of the Dreyfusard camp. The motives of the government leaders are clear enough: Loubet by inclination sought moderation, Galliffet was anxious to pacify the army while subjecting it to civilian rule, and Waldeck-Rousseau, eager to restore political tranquility but determined to rein in the most anti-Republican religious orders as part of his project of republican defense, needed to reassure Catholics.

However, the impassioned Fernand Labori saw amnesty as issuing from a conspiracy hatched by Waldeck and his friend Joseph Reinach, who persuaded a reluctant Mathieu to agree with it, as well as the more moderate—and more Catholic—lawyer retained by the Dreyfus family, Demange. Picquart was vehemently opposed because he wanted "to demonstrate that the charges brought against me are based on fraud and deception," and Labori—and Clemenceau—told the Dreyfus family they owed Picquart the right to clear his name. Zola too objected, and even Alfred Dreyfus initially hesitated (but pulled back from active opposition to complete the writing of his memoirs). If enacted, the amnesty would stop du Paty's indictment, drop the charges against Mercier and Esterhazy, but prevent Picquart and Zola from pursuing legal exoneration. (An exception was made for Dreyfus, who could continue the fight for legal rehabilitation.) Waldeck acknowledged the legitimacy of their complaints but persuasively argued that an amnesty "does not judge, nor does it accuse, nor does it exonerate, nor does it condemn [but] draws its inspiration from the public interest." By the end of 1900, to the dismay of the Dreyfusards, both houses of Parliament passed the measure. Following is part of the letter sent by Labori to Mathieu Dreyfus condemning the bill and an excerpt from Labori's newspaper article drawing a distinction between a pardon and an amnesty.

Document 14
Labori Protests Against an Amnesty
The Letter to Mathieu

The amnesty "covering all deeds relating to the Dreyfus Affair" is perhaps the most deplorable and scandalous measure that has been taken in three years. Especially since it is the work, I'm not saying of the republican party, but of the government of republican defense which the Dreyfus Affair brought to power. Certainly, no one more than myself, if I were simply considering my personal interest, would derive material advantage from amnesty. But to allow the passage of this law of iniquity, impotence, and deception without doing everything possible to oppose it, and whatever, moreover, the result of such effort be, seems to me not only an unjustifiable attitude, but an unpardonable error. . . .

The Newspaper Article

In accepting his pardon, Alfred Dreyfus did in no way acknowledge his guilt. For reasons it is not up to me to judge, he preferred his immediate freedom to the uninterrupted, heroic continuation of the efforts to achieve his political rehabilitation. Although he owes his salvation solely to a group of men joined by their interest in justice for all and concerned above all with pursuing a labor of social progress, it is his right as a private individual. An individual can place himself above the justice of men, and who would deny that Alfred Dreyfus was well placed to find such justice contemptible? He may—satisfied with the judgment of his conscience and whatever be the interest of all—prefer his freedom to his legal honor. But in so doing he is acting as an isolated and independent individual, not as a man gripped by humane concerns and aware of the beauty of social duty. He is acting purely as an individual, not as a member of the human collective, in solidarity with his fellow men. At the same time, however great the role he played may have been, he is no longer representative of anything.

Source: Jean-Denis Bredin, *The Affair: The Case of Alfred Dreyfus* (New York: George Braziller, 1986), 446, 448–449.

The *Action Française* (French Action)

In the years following the Dreyfus Affair, disillusionment with Parliament was widespread on the left, particularly with the antilabor policies enforced by successive Radical governments. The far right was also disillusioned. The monarchist cause had been revived by nationalists during the Dreyfus Affair. It was most energetically pursued by the *Action Française* movement, which in 1908 transformed its publication of the same name from a bimonthly to a daily newspaper, a newspaper that originated as an anti-Dreyfusard publication. The organization was directed by the journalists Charles Maurras and Léon Daudet, men who fiercely denounced the democratic republic and, in the name of an "integral nationalism" that blamed French misfortunes on such foreign elements as Jews and Freemasons, called for the return of the monarchy. Foreigners had spoiled the French race; Jews, Protestants, and other *métèques* (inferiors) prevented France from achieving true greatness; and national renewal could take place only by expelling these alien influences. Henry, Maurras argued, was the victim of a "Syndicate of Traitors" and as a great patriot had to be avenged. Founded in 1898 to fight the Dreyfusards, the *Action Française* movement soon came under Maurras's leadership. Intensely nationalistic, he made use of monarchism and Catholicism as vehicles to reestablish a France for the French alone. Still, he was to welcome France's defeat in 1940 and the collapse of the French Republic as providing the long-sought opportunity for national regeneration and a more highly structured society. The third issue of the revamped newspaper contained a declaration of principles for the movement it represented.

Document 15
The Principles of the *Action Française*
(Translated by the author)

The *Action Française* is the newspaper of good citizens disillusioned with the Republic and rallied to the Monarchy. . . .

The Republic is evil.

The Republic is the government of the Jews; the treacherous Jews like Ullmo and Dreyfus; the thieving Jews like Baron Jacques de Reinach; the Jews corrupting the people and persecuting the Catholic religion, like the Jewish inventor of the divorce law, and the Jewish inventor of the law of separation.

The Republic is the government of Protestant pedagogues who import from Germany, England, and Switzerland an educational system that besots and disconcerts the brains of French youth.

The Republic is the government of Freemasons, who only have one hatred, the Church; only one love, sinecures and the public treasury; instigators of civil war, religious war, social war, and financial parasites, they lead us to the material and moral bankruptcy that will ruin the investor and the worker, the merchant and the peasant, the functionary and the voter.

The Republic is the government of the more or less naturalized foreigners of metics [resident aliens], who recently polluted the converted Panthéon with the corpse of their Zola; they will monopolize the soil of France; they compete with workers of French blood for their just salary; they have laws voted which ruin our industry, forcing capital to emigrate and placing our resources in the service of Edward VII [the british king] and William II [the German emperor]. Doing its best for the Foreigner, the Republic endows us with every schism, harassing or threatening he who performs or creates labor; it is also *the government that has spilled the most workers' blood in Europe.* As soon as the Proletariat asks it to keep some of its innumerable promises, it replies with sword thrusts and rifle shots. . . .

WE WILL REPLACE IT WITH THE KING!

The King; that is, *France* personified by the descendant and heir of forty chiefs who have made, enlarged, maintained, and developed her. That the government of the King is the natural government of the nation is established by the simplest facts, like the testimony of the greatest masters of science and thought today. . . .

No patriot has the right to remain ignorant of the fact that in regard to social organization, the labor question, and decentralization, our Prince has delivered the key to the problem. *To reform in order to conserve: this is our entire program.*

French patriots, nationalists, anti-Dreyfusards, Catholics—men of order, men of progress—rich, poor, of all classes, of all trades, all parties; you have had enough, who are weary of complaining, who want to bring an end to it:

You will read every *Action Française*, which will present every day not only public wrongs but the MEANS, the sure means, the radical means, the only means of ending the miseries of the country.

OVERTHROW THE REPUBLIC!

PROCLAIM THE DUKE OF ORLÉANS!

Source: *L'Action Française*, March 23, 1908.

The Zionist Response

Theodor Herzl was a Hungarian Jew sent to Paris by the Vienna newspaper *Neue Frei Presse* in 1891. These were the years of the Panama scandal and the start of the Dreyfus Affair. The vicious anti-Semitism that he saw in the city he regarded as the center of civilization strengthened his conviction that assimilation, so optimistically acclaimed along with the development of liberal attitudes toward Jews in the eighteenth and nineteenth centuries, was doomed to fail given the rise of racial nationalism in the late nineteenth century. Legal guarantees of civil rights had not made them or other minorities equal and free, and if Jews were subject to so much hatred even in a country as enlightened as France, their only hope lay in securing a homeland of their own, that is, a Jewish national state (Zion). He developed his ideas in an important pamphlet, *Der Judenstaat* (The Jewish State), published in 1896. The following year Herzl organized the first Zionist World Congress in Basel, Switzerland. He would serve as its president until his death in 1904. Herzl did not create Zionism, but he transformed a comatose concept into a mass movement and a political force. Most of the leading Dreyfusards—and for that matter, most French and European intellectuals (Bernard-Lazare proved an important exception)—rejected the Zionist assertion that assimilation had not worked. Some of the less sympathetic condemned Zionist "racism," and even Bernard-Lazare never considered settling in Palestine. Joseph Reinach, for one, was horrified that Zionism should result from the effort to render justice to Dreyfus.

Document 16
The Jewish State and the Zionist Program

The Jewish question still exists. It would be foolish to deny it. It is a misplaced piece of medievalism which civilised nations do not seem able to shake off, try as they will. . . . The Jewish question persists wherever Jews live in appreciable numbers. Wherever it does not exist, it is brought in by Jewish immigrants. . . . I consider the Jewish question neither a social nor a religious one, even though it sometimes takes these and other forms. It is a national question. . . .

We have sincerely tried everywhere to merge with the national communities in which we live, seeking only to preserve the faith of our fathers. It is not permitted to us. In vain are we loyal patriots, sometimes super-loyal; in vain do we make the same sacrifices of life and property as our fellow citizens; in vain do we strive to enhance the fame of our native land in the arts and sciences, or her wealth by trade and commerce. In our native lands where we have lived for centuries we are still decried as aliens, often by men whose ancestors had not yet come at a time when Jewish sighs had long been heard in the country. The majority decides who the "alien" is; this, and all else in the relations between peoples, is a matter of power. . . . In the world as it now is and will probably remain, for the indefinite period, might takes precedence over right. It is without avail, therefore, for us to be loyal patriots, as were the Huguenots, who were forced to emigrate. If we were left in peace. . . . But I think we shall not be left in peace. . . .

A more serious objection would be that I am giving aid and comfort to the anti-Semites when I say we are a people—one people. Or that I am hindering the assimilation of Jews where there are hopes of achieving it, and endangering it where it is already an accomplished fact, insofar as it is possible for a solitary writer to hinder or endanger anything.

This objection will be brought forward especially in France. It will probably also be made in other countries, but I shall first answer only the French Jews, who afford the most striking example of my point.

However much I may esteem personality—powerful individual personality in statesmen, inventors, artists, philosophers, or leaders, as well as the collective personality of a historic group of human beings, which we designate "nation"—however much I may esteem personality, I do not mourn its decline. Whoever can, will, and must perish, let him perish. But the distinctive nationality of the Jews neither can, will, nor must perish. It cannot, because external enemies consolidate it. It does not wish to; this it has proved through two millennia of appalling suffering. It need not; that, as a descendant of countless Jews who refused to despair, I am trying once more to prove in this pamphlet. Whole branches of Jewry may wither and fall away. The tree lives on.

Hence, if any or all of French Jewry protest against this scheme, because they are already "assimilated," my answer is simple: The whole thing does not concern them at all. They are Israelitic Frenchmen? Splendid! This is a private affair for Jews alone.

However, the movement for the creation of the State which I here propose would harm Israelitic Frenchmen no more than it would harm those who have "assimilated" in other countries. It would, rather, be distinctly to their advantage. For they would no longer be disturbed in their "chromatic function," as Darwin puts it, but would be able to assimilate in peace, because present-day anti-Semitism would have been stopped for all time. For it would certainly be believed that they are assimilated to the very depths of their being if they remained in their old homes, even after the new Jewish State, with its superior institutions, had become a reality. . . .

It might further be said that we ought not to create new distinctions between people; we ought not to raise fresh barriers, we should rather make the old ones disappear. I say that those who think in this way are amiable visionaries; and the Homeland idea will go on flourishing long after the dust of their bones will have been scattered without trace by the winds. Universal brotherhood is not even a beautiful dream. Conflict is essential to man's highest efforts.

Well, then? The Jews, in their own State, will likely have no more enemies, and in their prosperity they will decline and dwindle, so that the Jewish people will soon disappear altogether? I imagine that the Jews will always have sufficient enemies, just as every other nation. . . .

Let me repeat once more my opening words: The Jews who will it shall achieve their State.

We shall live at last as free men on our own soil, and in our own homes peacefully die. . . .

And whatever we attempt there for our own benefit will redound mightily and beneficially to the good of all mankind.

Source: *Der Judenstaat*, trans. Arthur Hertzberg in *The Zionist Idea* (New York: Doubleday, 1959), 208–209, 211–212, 223, 225–226.

GLOSSARY OF
SELECTED TERMS

Bordereau: The manuscript document at the heart of the legal proceedings, the evidence on which Dreyfus was condemned, and which was endlessly evoked by the actors in the drama. It was a list of the information (on the hydraulic brake of the 120 millimeter cannon, artillery formation, manual of fire) promised by the author to the German military attaché, Maximilien von Schwartzkoppen.

Council of War *(Conseil de Guerre):* The deliberating body in the three courts-martial that comprised the Dreyfus Affair. The first convened in Paris on December 19, 1899, and three days later found Dreyfus guilty of treason; the second took place January 10 and 11, 1898, and acquitted Esterhazy; and the third, held at Rennes from August 8 until September 9, 1899, again found Dreyfus guilty and sentenced him to ten years' detention (a decision at once rescinded by presidential pardon). The first two councils were held behind closed doors, and each was composed of seven military judges.

Devil's Island *(Ile du Diable):* The island off the coast of Guinea where Dreyfus was condemned to "perpetual deportation"and spent four and a half years. Conditions were severe and worsened when rumors of his escape prompted the authorities to enclose his hut with two encircling fences and to keep the prisoner chained to his bed at night. His health deteriorated under such treatment.

Evidence *(Les Preuves):* On August 7, 1898, Jean Jaurès, defeated in the legislative elections held the previous May, began to publish a series of articles in the socialist newspaper *La Petite République*. By rigorously examining the published documents, he demonstrated that

Dreyfus could not have been guilty of the crimes for which he was convicted. In September, the articles were published as a book entitled *Les Preuves.*

Fort Chabrol: The anti-Semitic agitator Jules Guèrin, aware that charges had been brought against him and other nationalist leaders, took refuge with about fifteen friends in a house at 51 rue Chabrol, the headquarters of his Anti-Semitic League. The head of the government, Waldeck-Rousseau, hesitated to launch an attack and preferred to have the police lay siege to the house. For forty days, until September 19, 1899, the besieged held out, supplied by parcels of food thrown by sympathizers from the tops of passing buses. The episode took on a farcical dimension, and the expression "to hold a Fort Chabrol" (to be ridiculous) became a common figure of speech.

Henry Forgery *(faux Henry)*: The document that seemed to confirm Dreyfus's guilt was fabricated by Major Henry. He added the following sentence to a letter from Panizzardi to Schwartzkoppen sent in October 1898: "I read that a Deputy is going to raise questions concerning Dreyfus. If anyone in Rome asks for new explanations, I am going to say that I never had any ties to this Jew." Henry admitted his forgery on August 30, 1898, and a few days later killed himself in his prison cell.

Intellectuals *(Intellectuels)*: A word, used as a noun, that frequently appeared after January 1898. Clemenceau popularized it in an article in his newspaper, *L'Aurore*, when he congratulated the scholars, artists, and professors who had earlier signed a petition calling for the Dreyfus case to be reopened.

Opportunists: Conservative republicans who supported the constitutional laws of 1875 that divided power between the legislative and executive branches but who preferred to wait for the "opportune" time before voting for controversial legislation. They consequently downplayed the importance of social legislation but favored colonial campaigns and the secularization of education. Opportunists controlled government for much of the 1880s and 1890s. In the mid-1890s, they changed their name to "Progressists."

Ordinary Path *(Voie ordinaire)*: A phrase referring to the activities of the French cleaning woman, Madame Bastian, who retrieved the contents of the wastebasket in Schwartzkoppen's office, concealed them on her person, and brought them to French Intelligence. By such means, the *bordereau* was discovered and the *petit-bleu* came to Picquart's attention.

Petit-Bleu: In March 1896, the Statistical Section (the French intelligence service) received torn fragments of a special-delivery letter (written on thin blue paper) taken from Schwartzkoppen's office. Never sent, it was addressed to Esterhazy and revealed the existence of a French officer who was selling military secrets. The new head of the section, Lieutenant-Colonel Georges Picquart, noted that the handwriting matched that of the *bordereau*. In 1897, Major Henry forged telegrams in an effort to show that it was Picquart who sent the *petit-bleu* as part of a conspiracy to inculpate Esterhazy.

Radicals: Left-wing republicans who until the end of the 1880s preferred to concentrate power in a one-house assembly. They were initially more inclined to support measures of social legislation, rejected colonial wars as wasting resources better spent on preparing for a war of revenge against Germany, and supported anticlerical legislation. With Socialist votes, they came to dominate governments from 1899 until the outbreak of war in 1914.

Revisionists *(Révisionnistes)*: The name given, beginning in 1897, to those convinced of Dreyfus's innocence or persuaded that the 1894 court-martial was filled with irregularities. They joined forces to ask for a revision of the verdict by reopening the case. The term is largely synonymous with Dreyfusards.

Socialist Manifesto *(Manifeste Socialiste)*: On June 19, 1898, the Socialist deputies in the French Parliament, led by Jules Guesde and Edouard Vaillant, and initially supported by Jean Jaurès, denounced the Opportunists and clericals as two rival branches of the same bourgeois family and urged the proletariat to remain neutral in the Dreyfus Affair, dismissed as a "bourgeois civil war." Soon, a faction led by the labor leader Jean Allemane and then Jaurès himself broke with this strategy and joined the Dreyfusard campaign.

Statistical Section *(Section Statistique)*: The name used to designate the French intelligence service. At the time of Dreyfus's arrest, it was headed by Lieutenant-Colonel Sandherr, later by the newly promoted Lieutenant-Colonel Picquart.

Syndicate *(Syndicat):* The term used by opponents of revision, the anti-Dreyfusards, to characterize the Dreyfusard leadership, which they charged was being supplied with "Jewish gold" *(l'or juif).* On December 1, 1897, Zola published an article in *Le Figaro* entitled "Syndicate" in which he attacked the authors responsible for this allegation. The term was also used by Dreyfusards to designate what they perceived as a Jesuit-led reactionary conspiracy.

ANNOTATED BIBLIOGRAPHY

The works on the Dreyfus Affair are numerous, and new studies continue to appear. For those who read French, there are two inventories of books. One published near the end of the Affair is that of Paul Desachy, *Bibliographie de l'Affaire Dreyfus* (Paris: Cornely, 1905). A later inventory was published by Léon Lipschutz, *Bibliographie thématique et analytique de l'Affaire Dreyfus* (Paris: Fasquelle, 1970). The annual edition of the *Bibliographie annuelle de l'histoire de France* (Paris: Editions du Centre national de la recherche scientifique, 1964–) lists all books and articles on all aspects of French history published in all languages. There is a remarkably comprehensive and thematically organized bibliography appended to Jean-Denis Bredin's *The Affair: The Case of Alfred Dreyfus* (New York: George Braziller, 1986). A shorter bibliography (in English) than that of Desachy and Lipschutz is by Frederick Busi, "Bibliographical Overview of the Dreyfus Affair," *Jewish Social Studies* 40 (1978): 25–40. One other work, in French, must be mentioned: that of Joseph Reinach, *Histoire de l'Affaire Dreyfus*, 7 vols. (Paris: La Revue Blanche for vol. 1 and Fasquelle for the rest, 1901–1911). In spite of his role as an active Dreyfusard, Reinach's work is essential. Although he has erred with regard to Henry's role and his insistence on a Jesuit plot, Reinach is rich and rewarding. Not only is his book based on firsthand knowledge, but he also has made use of all the sources available to him, including his own papers. The index, volume 7, identifies almost all of the personalities involved. What follows is a selected list of English-language books on the Dreyfus Affair and its context. It should be consulted together with the Chapter 5 "The Dreyfus Affair in History."

Bredin, Jean-Denis. *The Affair: The Case of Alfred Dreyfus*. New York: George Braziller, 1986. The best lengthy study in English. It addresses not only the Dreyfus case but contains a superb analysis of the economic, social, and religious contexts at the turn of the century. A lawyer himself, Bredin presents the legal complexities in a highly readable manner. He rejects conspiracy theses, particularly that of the "third man," and notes the internal divisions within each camp as well as the similarities between them. This sensitive and skilled work questions whether the forces of reaction were really defeated.

Burns, Michael. *Dreyfus: A Family Affair, 1789–1945*. New York: HarperCollins, 1991. In this very readable book, Burns shows the impact of the Affair on the entire Dreyfus family. Through a history of the family, he provides a history of French Jewry from emancipation to the assimilation that made possible upward mobility and integration, at least of upper- middle-class Jews who consequently displayed their patriotism. Much of the book focuses on Mathieu's role in keeping his brother's case in the public eye and on a detailed account of Alfred's years in prison. The family history opens with Alfred's great-grandfather, a kosher butcher, and ends with Alfred's granddaughter participating in the Resistance and dying in Auschwitz.

Burns, Michael. *Rural Society and French Politics: Boulangism and the Dreyfus Affair*. Princeton, N.J.: Princeton University Press, 1984. Making extensive use of archival material in and outside Paris, Burns charts the reception of the Boulangist movement in rural France and concludes that it had an impact on rural France when it coincided with local concerns. This was also true of the Dreyfus Affair, but the case there is not made as strongly.

Cahm, Eric. *The Dreyfus Affair in French Society and Politics*. New York: Longman, 1996. Very good on the role of particular political, social, and intellectual groups and organizations in the period 1871–1914. Portraits of the leading personalities and a fresh translation of key sources supplement the narrative.

Chapman, Guy. *The Dreyfus Case: A Reassesssment*. London: Rupert Hart-Davis, 1955. A revisionist account that condemns the Dreyfusards (defined as opportunists who exploited their victory) yet still finds the anti-Dreyfusard stand false and is sympathetic to the church and the army, which because of their diversity cannot be considered as unified monoliths. The army is seen as nonpolitical, the church as less hostile, and anti-Semitism as a product of the press campaign. Not coincidentally, Chapman underestimates the moral dimension of the Dreyfus Affair. See the discussion in Chapter 5 of this book.

Derfler, Leslie. *Alexandre Millerand: The Socialist Years*. Paris and The Hague: Mouton, 1977. An account of the early career of the socialist leader who accepted a post in the Dreyfusard government of "republican defense" that tried to put an end to the Affair. The author argues that Socialist objections to the entry into the government of Millerand, the first Socialist to participate in a regularly established (as contrasted to a revolutionary) ministry, issued from private as well as ideological motives and that Millerand remained consistent with his "reformist" agenda while his party moved to the left.

Dreyfus Alfred. *Five Years of My Life, 1894–1899*. New York: McClure, Phillips, 1901.

———. *The Letters of Captain Alfred Dreyfus to His Wife*. New York: Harper & Row, 1899. The account of the Affair through the eyes of the victim. Obviously they are strongest on the torment he suffered as a prisoner on Devil's Island. These remain the source of all the primary accounts describing what happened to Dreyfus from his arrest until after the Rennes trial.

Du Gard, Roger Martin. *Jean Barois*. New York: Viking Press, 1949. An early novel by the Nobel Prize winner that conveys the ferment of the generation of the 1890s. In tracing the intellectual development of the leading protagonist, the writer gives an almost day-by-day account of the Dreyfus Affair, its impact, and its consequences.

Goldberg, Harvey. *The Life of Jean Jaurès*. Madison: University of Wisconsin Press, 1962. The best biography of the great Socialist leader in English (and perhaps in any other language). Written with passion and verve, it shows how Jaurès brought his party, hitherto neutral, to the defense of the rich army officer condemned by his peers. The differences between Jaurès and other Socialists come through clearly.

Griffiths, Richard. *The Use of Abuse: The Polemics of the Dreyfus Affair and its Aftermath*. Oxford: Berg, 1991. A discussion of the most important writers involved in the Affair that analyzes the rhetorical devices in the polemics—especially in the press but on the part of intellectuals as well. Griffiths argues that a "polemical culture" existed in turn-of-the-century France and that Dreyfusards and anti-Dreyfusards used the same rhetorical techniques. For example, while one side blamed a "Jewish plot," the other blamed a "Jesuit plot."

Halasz, Nicholas. *Captain Dreyfus: The Story of a Mass Hysteria*. A fast-moving account with emphasis placed on the public's response to the unfolding drama, however, the scholarly analysis is less powerful than the narration. See the extended discussion of Halasz's book in Chapter 5 of this book.

Hoffman, Robert. *More than a Trial: The Struggle over Captain Dreyfus*. New York: Free Press, 1980. The familiar story is told, but the author goes on to discuss what he calls the "artifacts of the struggle": the newspaper articles, the speeches, posters, cartoons, photographs, novels, plays, and even toys and games. More than a trial, the Affair was a "civil war" and serves as a prism for French history. Much of the anti-Dreyfusard hostility is seen as "a rage against things modern."

Hyman, Paula. *The Jews of Modern France*. Berkeley: University of California Press, 1998. Using a wide variety of sources, Hyman explores the nature of anti-

Semitism in France, from the *ancien régime* to the present, and specifically the choices Jews faced in defining their identity. Very good on the Zionist challenge to assimilation.

Jennings, Jeremy, ed. *Intellectuals in Politics: From the Dreyfus Affair to Salman Rushdie.* New York: Routledge, 1997. Fourteen essays by historians and other scholars that explain the role of intellectuals, as it is and how it should be, and their relationship with scholars and politicians. They must not be spokesmen for the state or elitists out of touch with the larger population.

Johnson, Douglas. *France and the Dreyfus Affair.* New York: Walker, 1966. A good analysis of the legal and military aspects of the case. Although sometimes indulgent toward the General Staff, Johnson is scrupulous and reliable. There is little on Dreyfus's character; this book is rather a study of the context. A consequence of the Affair was to turn attention away from concrete issues to ideological symbols.

Johnson, Martin P. *The Dreyfus Affair: Honour and Politics in the Belle Epoque.* New York: St. Martin's Press, 1999. A good, short popular account that takes into consideration the latest research on the Affair. In spite of the title, it offers less on the *belle époque* than on the affair.

Kaplan, Robert Elliot. *Forgotten Crisis: The Fin-de-Siècle Crisis of Democracy in France.* Oxford: Berg, 1995. The "forgotten crisis" was the struggle to pass an income tax. The established forces of society were terrified by the prospect. It was the Dreyfusard "revolution" that finally defeated this "Jacobin socialist" threat inasmuch as the Radicals who supported the Waldeck-Rousseau government used the Dreyfus Affair to justify the government's opposition to the tax they no longer defended. Kaplan also insists the army used Esterhazy as a double agent to deceive the Germans. These theses are interesting, but lack hard evidence to sustain them.

Kedward, Roderick. *The Dreyfus Affair: Catalyst for Tensions in French Society.* London: Longmans, 1965. Provides a series of documents in the original French, with useful introductions in English. There are good discussions of the political and religious contexts. Students are encouraged to deal with the problems raised by the documents and are made aware of the wider perspectives.

Kleeblatt, Norman. *The Dreyfus Affair: Art, Truth and Justice.* Berkeley: University of California Press, 1987. The catalog of a 1987 exhibition arranged by the Jewish Museum of New York City that also contains interesting essays by specialists in French history, including Benjamin Martin on the legal system, Michael Marrus on popular anti-Semitism, Paula Hyman on the French Jewish community, and Susan Suleiman on the literary significance of the Dreyfus Affair. The book contains many illustrations of the iconography of the Affair in its exploration of anti-Semitism and of the intellectuals and artists who were for and against Dreyfus.

Larkin, Maurice. *Church and State after the Dreyfus Affair*. New York: Harper & Row, 1974. The Dreyfusard anticlerical campaign led to the separation of church and state, but the Combes government wanted to retain the Concordat. Both miscalculations by Combes, who believed he could force Vatican concessions, and the pressure of his Socialist allies, who hoped that separation would remove anticlericalism as an issue, explain why separation happened. Larkin makes good use of archival sources and Combes's private papers.

Lewis, David Levering. *Prisoners of Honor: The Dreyfus Affair*. New York: Morrow, 1973. A well-written, popular, and well-researched introduction. Lewis was one of the first historians to make use of family interviews, the Esterhazy papers, and the "secret dossier" long buried in the army's archives. He breaks with those who write about the Affair "without Dreyfus" and focuses on the unfortunate victim and the judicial proceedings. He sees the Affair as a human tragedy and all its actors as "prisoners of honor." In so doing, he minimizes the political and social context.

Lindemann, Albert S. *The Jew Accused: Three Anti-Semitic Affairs (Dreyfus, Belis, Frank), 1894–1915*. New York: Cambridge University Press, 1991. The famous cases of three falsely accused Jews. Each affair is put in its national and historical context. The author concludes that although anti-Semitism was present in all of the trials, it played no decisive role in any of them. The story is also one of non-Jews who disliked Jews but nevertheless showed respect for justice and truth.

Malino, Frances, and Bernard Wasserstein, eds. *The Jew in Modern France*. Hanover, NH: University Press of New England, 1985. A series of essays that focus on French anti-Semitism. Eugen Weber's dismisses the relevance of the Jewish question in French society ("Jews are simply humanity writ large"). Still, most essays deal with it and provide some basic tools for the study of modern French Jewry. The themes are those of assimilation and anti-Semitism.

Marrus, Michael. *The Politics of Assimilation: The Jewish Community in France at the Time of the Dreyfus Affair*. Oxford: Oxford University Press, 1971. Marrus argues that emancipation shattered the Jewish community but provided individual Jews with opportunities and a less dangerous life for all—hence, their loyalty to and trust in the government. He concludes that the politics of assimilation were bankrupt but finds it difficult to offer alternatives.

Paléologue, Maurice. *My Secret Diary of the Dreyfus Affair, 1894–1899*. London: Secker and Warburg, 1957. The English translation of the author's account of the trials and public perception of them, seen from his perspective at the Ministry of Foreign Affairs. Charged with keeping watch on developments, Paléologue was converted to the Dreyfusard cause. He exaggerates his own role and insists on the "third man" thesis, but he spoke with the chief characters and offers an interesting, if gossipy, account.

Silvera, Alain. *Daniel Halévy and His Times*. Ithaca, N.Y.: Cornell University Press, 1966. An intellectual who epitomized his times, Halévy broke with the Socialists and Radicals who exploited the Dreyfus Affair. By citing the responses of such writers as Georges Sorel and Maurras, Silvera evokes the intellectual atmosphere in Paris at the turn of the century.

Snyder, Louis., ed. *The Dreyfus Case: A Documentary History*. New Brunswick, N.J.: Rutgers University Press, 1973. Translations of the more important documents concerning the Affair with useful narrative introductions.

Sonn, Richard, D. *Anarchism and Cultural Politics in Fin-de-Siècle France*. Lincoln: University of Nebraska Press, 1989. Examines the interaction of artistic and intellectual life in Paris in the 1890s, with vitality rather than decadence as the theme. Although anarchists constituted a minority among artists, as in the working class, their ideas had a greater impact than their numbers would suggest because of prevailing liberalism.

Steevens, G. W. *The Tragedy of Dreyfus*. London: Harper and Brothers, 1899. Steevens was a newspaper reporter who attended the Rennes trial, the focal point of his book. He provides the colorful details that only an observant eye-witness can offer, as well as excellent portraits of the leading characters.

Sternhell, Zeev. *The Birth of Fascist Ideology*. Princeton, N.J.: Princeton University Press, 1994. There was a fascist ideology that needs to be taken seriously. It emerged as a revolt against the materialistic positivism at the end of the nineteenth century and seduced European intellectuals, both left and right, in France and Italy. Sternhell's critics, point out that not all antiliberals and antiparliamentarians were fascist and that fascist ideas needed the stimulus of World War I and economic depression to be translated into action.

Sutton, Michael. *Nationalism, Positivism, and Catholicism: The Politics of Charles Maurras and French Catholics (1890–1914)*. Cambridge: Cambridge University Press, 1983. A journalist, a polemicist, and the "founding ideologue of the Action Française," Maurras was far from being a solitary scholar. Speeches, Maurrassian ideology, including his anti-Semitism and romanticism, and the Catholic reaction to it highlight this book.

Watson, David Robin. *Georges Clemenceau: A Political Biography*. London: Eyre Metheun, 1974. The best biography in English of the French statesman and the first full-length scholarly biography in any language. It is not a well-rounded portrait, but it is authoritative and exhaustive. For Watson, Clemenceau, despite his faults, would guarantee that France would remain a liberal and democratic society. His role in the Affair is covered objectively and dispassionately.

Weber, Eugen. *France: Fin de Siècle*. Cambridge, Mass.: Harvard University Press, 1986. Weber provides a lively portrait of an era. His themes are sport, fashion, gossip, and, of course, sociopolitical crises such as the Dreyfus Affair.

This is social history—art, theater, inventions, the press—but somewhat disjointed and confusing to read.

Wilson, Nelly. *Bernard-Lazare: Anti-Semitism and the Problem of Jewish Identity in Late Nineteenth-Century France.* Cambridge: Cambridge University Press, 1978. In the first English-language biography of Lazare, Wilson sets out to rescue him from undeserved historical anonymity and place him at the center of literary anarchism, the Dreyfus Affair, and Zionism. She overstates the case in arguing that Dreyfus owed his freedom to Lazare but recognizes the crucial role he played in creating a "moral syndicate" working on the accused's behalf.

Wilson, Stephen. *Ideology and Experience: Anti-Semitism in France at the Time of the Dreyfus Affair.* Rutherford, N.J.: Fairleigh Dickinson University Press, 1982. In contrast to Burns's *Rural Society and French Politics*, Wilson argues that anti-Semitism was widely diffused in urban areas of France. Hailed as "one of the most important works on anti-Semitism in many years," his book tries to see what made writers and agitators strike out against Jews. Using police archives and anthropological studies, Wilson identifies different types of anti-Semitism, including economic and even sexual, and seeks to understand the phenomenon by exploring its social functions.

Zola, Emile. *The Dreyfus Affair: "J'accuse" and Other Writings.* Edited by Alain Pagès. New Haven, Conn.: Yale University Press, 1996. An English translation of Zola's writings on the Dreyfus Affair, including newspaper articles and correspondence.

A Note on Internet Sources

There are several Internet sites under the heading, "Dreyfus Affair." Most contain brief summaries, encyclopedia articles, copies of Zola's famous letter, and some photographs and cartoons. Because old sites disappear and new ones emerge, some of the following Web sites may no longer be in existence and others may have appeared after this book was submitted for publication. It is advisable to type "Dreyfus Affair" in the search box of various browsers such as Yahoo!, Google, Lycos, and Metacrawler.

http://www.georgetown.edu/guieu/dnews.html   This site, arranged by a Georgetown University professor, Jean-Max Guyieu, provides a chronology of events, Zola's letter, iconography, photographs, an advertisement for the professor's "Comprehensive Digital Bibliography of the Dreyfus Affair" on CD-ROM, and links to papers presented on the Dreyfus Affair at a Georgetown University centennial conference held in February 1998 and a Columbia University colloquium held the same month. The papers are in English and in French, but not all are accessible on the Internet.

http://perso.magic.fr/themony/pascal/lois/jaccuse.html   A photograph of the first page of Clemenceau's newspaper, *L'Aurore*, containing Zola's letter.

http://www.france2.fr/evenement/jaccuse.html   A photograph of *L'Aurore*, and an extract of Zola's letter, a cartoon in the press, a chronology of events, and a summary of the Affair (all in French). Also has links to the full text of Zola's letter and books available electronically on the French National Library's "Gallica" site.

http://www.albion.edu/student/wank/engpaper.html   A brief summary of the Affair from a student, based on secondary sources and *New York Times* articles published in the 1890s. There are links to other Web sites.

http://www.wfu.edu/~sinclair/dreyfus.html   Two photos (of Dreyfus and Zola), a summary of the Affair, and the *Time Magazine* story of September 25, 1995, on the French army's conceding Dreyfus's innocence.

http://www.geocities.com/CapitolHill/8632   Another student Web page, with several short essays on the Affair.

http://www.dreyfusaffair.org   A time line and brief biographies of the leading characters.

http://JAJZ-ed.org.il   Synopses, an index of names, and a bibliography.

http://trc.ucdavis.edu/French/FRJV/html   An interesting course outline from the University of California at Davis on aspects of the Dreyfus Affair and Jewish history.

http://www.yahoo.com   Type in "Dreyfus Affair" for "Beyond the Pale," a history of the Affair that emphasizes anti-Semitism. There are numerous photographs and links to other sources. This site highlights the development of modern anti-semitism. Contains photographs (with comments) of Theodor Herzl, Alfred Dreyfus, the degradation ceremony, cartoons, Zola's family, the Rennes trial, and assorted posters.

Films

Given the development of motion pictures at the turn of the century and the passions unleashed by the Dreyfus Affair, it is scarcely surprising that early moviemakers sought to record as much as possible of what happened on film. They tried to photograph the Rennes trial and the leading personalities, invading their privacy and even faking scenes they could not record. Indeed, one film historian credits the Dreyfus Affair for the origins of the documentary, with all its attendant problems: invasion of privacy, fake footage, and censorship.[1] As early as August 1899, a pioneer cinematographer, Georges Mèliés, produced a fifteen-minute documentary.

Audiences erupted: fights broke out in the theaters showing the film, with spectators hurling objects at each other. The government thereupon banned the film and then banned the production of any other film on the Affair. Not until 1950 was this ban lifted, and not until 1974 did a French government allow a film to be made about the case. English-Language films include the following:

Prisoner of Honor. HBO Pictures, An Etude Product (movies made for television). 1991. Approximately 90 minutes. A well-acted film starring Richard Dreyfus (who plays Picquart) and directed by Ken Russell. A newspaper reporter visits Esterhazy in England in the 1920s, and in a series of flashbacks, the story of the Dreyfus Affair is told. Understandably Picquart's role is emphasized, while that of Mathieu is scarcely explored. In other respects, a remarkable degree of accuracy is achieved, and obviously the visual impact adds a dimension that cannot be reached by reliance on the written word alone.

The Life of Emile Zola. Warner Brothers Pictures, 1937. Approximately 90 minutes. Zola's life, from the experiences of the young writer to the famous novelist's struggles on behalf of Alfred Dreyfus, is portrayed in a film that received ten Academy Award nominations. In his own Oscar-nominated performance, Paul Muni plays Zola, and a distinguished cast portrays the other leading personalities in the Affair. Curiously, in spite of the importance of anti-Semitism in the Dreyfus Affair, the word *Jewish* is never used in the film.

The Dreyfus Case. British films, 1931. 90 minutes. Overshadowed by the more elaborate *Life of Emile Zola*, this more historically accurate British film, starring Cedric Hardwicke, provides a reasonably clear account of the famous case. When made, however, the film depicted events only thirty years in the past, and some still believed Dreyfus was guilty. Consequently, although the producers tried not to offend anyone, the film was not widely distributed in France (it could not have been made there) and not shown at all in countries where anti-Jewish sentiment prevailed.

I Accuse. Metro-Goldwyn-Mayer, 1957. 99 minutes. Starring José Ferrer, MGM's version of the trial, imprisonment, retrial, pardon, and exoneration satisfactorily rises to such great moments as the degradation and Zola's call to arms. The film was scripted by the writer Gore Vidal from Nicholas Halasz's book. For one critic, however, it skips over most of the ambiguities and paradoxes found in the Affair.

The Dreyfus Affair. University of Leeds Videotext. Written by David Coward. 35 minutes. Distributed by Video Forum, a division of Jeffrey Norton

Publishers, Guilford, Connecticut. Essentially a lecture by a university professor, making use of photographs, with some acting out of the dramatic moments, such as the degradation ceremony, of the Affair. A solid, objective introduction.

Note

1. Stephen Bottomore, "Dreyfus and Documentary," *Sight and Sound* 54 (Autumn 1984): 290–293.

INDEX

ABOUT THE AUTHOR

LESLIE DERFLER is a Professor of History at Florida Atlantic University. His most recent books are *Paul LaFargue and the Flowering of French Socialism, 1882–1911* (1998) and *An Age of Conflict: Readings in 20th Century European History* (2001).